T0207885

Creature Comforts
for Horses

Creature Comforts for Horses

Gwen Slade

CREATURE COMFORTS FOR HORSES

iUniverse books may be ordered through booksellers or by contacting:

iUniverse
1663 Liberty Drive
Bloomington, IN 47403
www.iuniverse.com
1-800-Authors (1-800-288-4677)

ISBN: 978-1-5320-0065-2 (sc)
ISBN: 978-1-5320-0066-9 (e)

Print information available on the last page.

iUniverse rev. date: 08/30/2016

$19.95 CAD

Callie, Foxy, Apache, PJ and hiding in the back the Catman!

Introduction

"There is something about the outside of a horse that is good for the inside of man"....Winston Churchill

"Creature Comforts for Horses" was born of a desire to turn complicated and difficult into a trouble-free, effortless understanding of the nutritional and daily care needs of our horses.

When the reality of adulthood takes control of our decision making, life then has a way of interfering with the best laid plans and intentions of childhood dreams and wishes.

More often than not, if the nurturing nest doesn't include a culture of horses, then the road travelled probably won't either. But a passion is a passion and as with any passion, it seems to simmer gentle just below the surface of our very being waiting for the stars to align and set it free.

That is exactly what happened to me. Memories are like little vignettes often triggered in our minds by significant or insignificant events that signal where we've been and can influence where we are going.

Events occurred that brought me to the cattle ranch of friends in Saskatchewan. They also raised appaloosa and quarter horses. A passion was rekindled when I bought my first horse. Before I knew it, and only few short years later, I found myself the proud owner of 7 horses. The magnificent 7 became my obsession.

The kindling of a long buried passion became a warm welcoming state of well being found in the calm, contented peaceful serenity of an environment created by horses. It becomes a refreshing rejuvenating oasis, a retreat if you will, from the hectic stressful demands of today's world. I had found my state of balance.

I can ride, but I'm not a world champion. Honestly, I'm not even a local champion but I can stay in the saddle. Whether on the ground taking care of their needs or sitting on the back of one of my very patient, gentle, tolerant babies, I am always afforded admission to their world of balance and harmony. A world grounded in the calm well being of oneness with oneself, one another and the universe.

But every family has "that" child and that would be my Ms Foxy Lady. Ms Foxy's life story is a tale for another time; suffice to say I bought Foxy as a bred mare that had to have her right eye removed because of neglect. Foxy is a great mother, sweet affectionate incurably nosey girl, a gentle giant puppy who willingly and quietly follows everywhere.

Ms Foxy takes the bit, bridle and saddle with casual indifference but the minute any rider puts a foot in the stirrup and starts the bounce of mounting she will turn her head and with her one eye look back at the rider. If a horse had eyebrows to arch, Ms Foxy would do so with ears flattening; a look that clearly telegraphs "seriously....don't do that". The very look she would give her daughter Callie when she was young and being a brat.

If ignored, then that comfortable settle in wiggle on the saddle suddenly becomes the hold on for dear life experience no one outside of a bronco rider would appreciate. I'm thinking this quirk was the very reason Ms Foxy was put up for sale. She is a gem with the farrier, to catch, to load, to tack up and will stand for hours for grooming. Just doesn't like passengers.

I love her and she is my go to girl when I am upset. Foxy seems to get the emotion and will calmly rub my hair with her nose and gently lie her head on my shoulder. I don't care if she prefers not to be ridden. She is ever so willing to give a "kiss" for a treat and sometimes just because. We have an understanding. She's my companion horse and I am her companion human. Ms Foxy has taught me to accept things for what they are and not so much for what I think they should be.

The reward I soon discovered become the reciprocated unexpected blessing of an unconditional love and an acceptance for who I am, with no validation required. It just doesn't get any better than that.

Me, Foxy, Catman and my stall companion, little Miss Missy

This is not a book about how to choose a horse. This is not a book about how to train a horse. Neither is it a book about how to ride a horse. It is a book about knowing your horse from the inside out. It is a book of information and guidance to the creature comforts of horses. It is a book of awareness, knowledge and understanding of an optimal state of wellness for our horses. A horse that does not feel well will not perform well.

It is a state of wellness that brings both the horse and rider to a common ground of trust, performance and appreciation.

This can only be achieved through the perceptive, insightful giving of nutritional food and all those creature comfort needs required for the love of the horse.

Be it a companion horse, a show celebrity or all those in between, doesn't matter, the basic creature comfort needs are all the same. Initially this book was to be a mini-cook book of horse treats and it just simply grew from there.

I began to realize when researching products I would need to make horse treats, it wasn't the treats that were making them just a little on the chubbie butt side. They didn't get enough to make that kind of impact.

To say a light bulb came on would be an exaggeration. Honestly it was more like the slow slide of a dimmer switch light revealing the fact "the less you know, the more you think you know" replaced with "the more you know; the more you realize how much you don't know".

Maybe I needed to take a look at what and how I was feeding my horses. Maybe I needed to understand how they digested food. Maybe I needed to be able to recognize how nutrients impact every aspect of my horse's well being. Maybe I needed to appreciate, 'we are what we eat' is as relevant to the horse as it is to the human.

The gathering of all this information for the betterment of my horses has been a passionate labour of love teaching me so much more than I ever knew. I am so thrilled to share it with you.

Dozens of trips to the library, bookstores and searching the internet together with hours of reading and listening to wise seasoned horse people and 20 years of on the job learning has culminated in the writing of 'Creature Comforts for Horses'.

For the past 25 years I have worked as a northern clinical practitioner in both First Nation's and Inuit communities in northern Canada. It was during those years of northern nursing that I began to appreciate the profound effect diet has on the health and welfare of the human condition.

I'm sure you are asking, what has this to do with horses? It has, as I soon began to discover, the same profound effect on the equine condition as it does on the human. "We are what we eat" is as equally relevant to our horses as it is to ourselves. Obesity is now considered one of the major disorders in the western world and the root evil of so many disease processes in both humans and horses.

I have witnessed firsthand, in both First Nations and Inuit communities, the metabolic chaos created when diets maintained for hundreds of years are suddenly changed to accommodate assimilation into an adopted modern life style.

For centuries the horse was free to wander and graze continually 14 – 16 hours a day. Things changed dramatically with domestication. Hundreds of years of metabolizing suddenly altered to accommodate modern harried lifestyles of most horse owners.

This is a book about the creature comforts for horses and, for the purposes of this book, the focus will be on the horse and not so much, the human.

History dictates the strength, durability and stamina of the horse has played a pivotal role in the evolution of mankind. From hieroglyphics on walls of rock; to covered wagons; to being the difference between conquered or conqueror in the matter of the First World War, or Secretariat, who validated for the blue colour working class the "little" guy can win.

The story 'War Horse', popular in print and on both live stage and big screen reveals the heroism of the horse during the First World War. Research into the role of the horse during the Great War reveals clearly without their courage, stamina and willingness to please, we may not have defeated the evil that threatened the free world. Wow! What a debt we owe.

I truly believe my passion for horses was sparked by a gentleman and his assistant that trucked through postwar suburbia with a camera and a pony. They single handily immortalized thousands of baby boomer infants and nameless ponies with the click of a Kodak camera. I loved sitting on that pony and I have the picture to prove it.

me circa 1948

Almost everyone, fleetingly or longingly, has at one time or another, felt the urge to ride a horse. Be it the 25 cent weather beaten mechanical steed at the front of the grocery store; or the broom, with two steps of passionate belief transforms into another Northern Dancer; or that unforgettable rocking horse found under the Christmas tree on the first Christmas remembered, mankind has shared an innate affinity with the horse on so many, many levels.

Food is at the heart of all mammal creature comfort needs. Two legged or four legged, it does not matter, healthy eating equates to optimal health and performance. It is my mission to bring awareness and understanding of how the same essential nutritional needs important to man are also vitally important to the horse.

Whether it is an intimate dinner party at the dining table or a gathering around the hay feeder, a state of well being is always created when good food, family and friends come together. A phenomenon of peace and harmony the horse has known and practiced for centuries.

Pasture alone often does not provide enough nutrients for horses; maybe for cows and goats, but not for horses. Consequently, horses are fed supplements in the form of concentrates (oats, corn, barley, beet pulp, soybean meal, etc), and hay but some concentrates can literally be considered 'fast foods' – full of energy in the form of sugars and starches.

I will discuss the need to recognize most horses are under worked and over-fed on "fast foods" which inevitably leads to obesity, health issues and behaviour problems.

We recognize this wicked trilogy in our children and ourselves when we access convenient foods from the grocery store and 'super size me' fast food restaurants. We have unwittingly become the 'junk food' generation because fast and convenient fits and supports our harried, tenured instant everything hectic lifestyles.

I absolutely love my horses. My horses are my passion and they most definitely occupy a very important portion of my family circle. You are reading my book so I know we are on the same page sharing the same infatuation for this most majestic animal.

Have I discovered that I am unwittingly guilty of practically killing my babies with kindness? That would be a resounding yes. Without warning I found myself the proud owner of hunkie chunkies and fatty patties. How did that happen?

Did I understand the eating disposition and habits of the equine world? Thought I did. I have discovered and come to understand I had a lot to learn. The writing of this book chronicles the learning curve I experienced on my journey to comprehending what I was doing wrong and how to turn uninformed into informed.

It is my hope and desire you will come to appreciate you will not know your horse until you know about your horse. If your horse does not feel well, he will not perform well and it won't matter your riding skill or your teaching prowess.

It is my hope and desire you will have awareness of the basic physiology and anatomy of the horse. It is my hope and desire you will recognize this is the first step toward knowing your horse, while understanding that the food digested is the next big step to bringing your horse to an optimal level of wellness.

It is my hope and desire you too can benefit from my quest to understand the healthy nutritional requirements and the daily creature comfort needs of the horse. And just as importantly, how to adapt this knowledge and awareness into the hectic harried lifestyles we all experience in this modern world of instant everything.

Prologue

With every trip through a book store, I continued my quest
to find "the one stop shop" book of information on needful
stuff for horse care. For me, knowing when, what and why
I should and shouldn't be feeding and deeding the needs
of my steeds would have been the best discover since King
Tuk's tomb. Just couldn't find a book that addressed the
creature comfort needs of my horse, so I decided to create
my own.

Creature Comforts for Horses will identify the fruits,
vegetables and vegetation that are a healthy supplement
to a horse's diet and as well identify those that are not
recommended for equine consumption.

This book will make every attempt to take the mystery out
of the science of nutrition. I will identify the nutritional
content and benefits found in fruits, vegetables, vegetation,
grains, hay and pasture forage and how this impacts the well
being of our horses.

After that, I have no trouble leaving everything else to the scientists. If not, this book runs the risk of becoming just another, 'more than I need to know', boring read.

Based on healthy nutritional choices, I have created easy to make/bake horse treat recipes your horse will appreciate with the 'more please' response. A confident statement made based on the testimony submitted by my, from time to time, pernickety crew.

Recipes so practical and easy, they invite the young riders to become aware of the value of good nutrition for the horse. The make/ bake recipes become a 'pay it forward' moment for you and the young horse lovers in your life circle.

Easy....I love easy. Truly, who doesn't love easy? Easy does not equate to lazy. Lazy is defined as 'unwilling to do any work or make an effort'. Easy is defined as 'uncomplicated, straightforward, trouble and stress-free'. Yes....I love easy.

All the attributes we looked for in a well balance horse. Not to mention, is this not the optimal state of mind we humans seek as we set out each day to secure our daily bread. Only the truly fortunate know, if uncomplicated and stress-free are not found during the daily pursuit of securing our daily bread, it will be found in the evening visit to the horse stalls.

In order to ensure my babies fit the definition of "healthy as a horse", many, many, many hours of research, reading and verifying information on the nutritional and daily care needs of our horses went into the writing of this book.

Creature Comforts for Horses may not necessarily give you the immediate answer you seek. But it does contain information that will help you, together with your veterinarian, farrier and/or other equine professional, to make informed decisions that will only enhance the creature comforts of your horse.

Today there is an increase in horse ownership and the horse has become a valued member of many more families. The average lifespan of 20 – 30 years identifies the ability to establish a long time 'life time' bond with a forever friend; a bond of a friendship that can only keep you forever young.

A couple of years after buying my first horse, I suddenly realized human anatomy and physiology may be my shtick but I truly knew nothing about the anatomy and physiology of the horse. That needed to be corrected if I was going to give the best care to my babies. What I learned was both informative and fascinating in my quest to give the best creature comfort care to my horses.

I also found that my "horsey" friends had a wealth of tips/hints for homeopathic remedies that simply needed to be in a quick and easy reference book. I am sure you will be familiar with many of these helpful tips/hints, but a review and the addition of something new and beneficial is always a bonus.

My mission in writing Creature Comforts for Horses was to help myself and others to better understand the basic physiology and anatomy of the horse. Then, and only then is the process of digestion understood and corroborates the when, why, what and how nutrition is considered and utilized by the body.

There is a confidence gained when we feel knowledgeable and aware. It cultivates a confidence that not only improves the overall health and performance of our horses, but also contributes to our own state of emotional wellness and performance when interacting with our horses. Knowledge builds confidence and confidence is a required motivator for the achievement of all our hopes and dreams.

I want to share with you one of my favourite quotes from a very remarkable woman. She was not a horse person by any stretch of the imagination. But she was a woman of immense courage and conviction who tore down stereotyping, broke through social barriers and confronted society with its double standards with a deliciously outrageous sense of humour.

"Don't follow any advise, no matter how good it is, unless you feel as deeply in your spirit as you think in your mind, that the counsel is wise"......**Joan Rivers.**

Words of advice I reference when confronted with information/instructions received in any given situation of uncertainty but most particularly in the care and interaction with my horses.

In hindsight we are all knowledgeable. How many times have you said to yourself, 'oh I knew I shouldn't have gone there'; or 'I knew I shouldn't have said that; or 'I knew I shouldn't have done that'.

Any decision that stirs an angst, hesitation, or tension is the rocky road. On the other hand, any decision that stirs a sense of wellbeing, decisiveness and ease is the smooth road even if it is contrary to the advice given.

I have learned the hard way to follow my spiritual intuition over the dictates of my mind and avoid the right to regret my decisions. Sometimes it's difficult to recall the mind often harbours a prejudice in its needful desire to please and gain approval of others while the honesty of intuition has no prejudice. In reality, on some days, this continues to be a work in progress as old habits die hard.

This book is not intended as the 'be all to end all' for the healthy eating for your horse. It is intended as an information source to start your own journey of discovery of an optimal nutritional feeding plan for your best friend's creature comfort needs.

The hope is always this shared information will afford you a platform from which to start your own research and also better allow you to make an informed and knowledge based decision when consulting with professionals.

The information shared in my book is not intended as a 'one size fits all' but rather can be used in conjunction and in consultation with your veterinarian, farrier and/or equine professional to meet any special need requirements essential to your horse's ability to enjoy optimal health and wellness.

The bonus, I soon began to discover, was just how closely so many nutritional needs required for a horse's well being aligned with those required for the rider/owner. Who would have thunk it! The bond between the human and the horse is found on so many levels of life.

The witnessed bond of trust, loyalty and love that develops between the quintessential prey animal, the horse and the quintessential predator, man is living proof miracles do happen. Those of us who have had our lives enriched by this miracle know we are blessed.

The more knowledge and awareness of the horse, the better we can care for and meet the creature comfort needs of this most magnificent of domesticated animals.

Sheighlyn and Blondie at the stalls

Just as it is with the human anatomy, the wellness of each system of your horse is dependent on the overall wellness of this powerful animal. It becomes a domino effect when one system becomes unbalanced. If not corrected, it will impact the wellness of other systems and organs until the general health and welfare of your horse is at risk.

Physiology and Anatomy of the Horse

Chapter 1

"Horse sense is the thing a horse has, which keeps it from betting on people."......W. C. Fields

FACTS ABOUT THE EARS

The ear of the horse is an incredible organ of efficiency. Not only are the ears an organ of balance, they are the ultimate communication instrument telegraphing the perception of what the horse is hearing. Horses are able to hear sounds at both higher and lower frequencies. Horses are very sensitive to the tone of our voices. We do not need to shout to be heard.

The horse's ears are one of the most expressive parts of a horse. Horses have 10 muscles that allow the ears to rotate 180 degrees exhibiting the expressive emotion of the moment; be it sociability, friendliness, apprehension, fear or anger. The ears can broadcast so much information to us about a horse's personality and mood.

The outer ear includes the pinna and the ear canal. The pinna is shaped to capture sound waves and funnel them through the ear canal to the eardrum. The pinnae can move independently of each other giving the horse the ability to locate multiple sounds at the same time.

The pinnae's function is to capture sound waves and funnel them into the external auditory canal to the middle ear. The auditory bones transmit the eardrum's resulting movements to the inner ear. The inner ear, which includes auditory nerve, cochlea and labyrinth, transfers the sound waves into nerve impulses which are sent to the brain's hearing centre.

And that, in a nutshell, is how a horse can go from 0 to 100 in a nanno-second or calmly follows like a puppy dog. Just keep your eyes on those ears. The ears tell all.

The good news is horses are not susceptible to many ear problems. Insect-induced dermatitis of the ears is the most common concern and will present as scabby ears with obvious bug bites and sometimes localized swelling.

Insect-induced dermatitis is fairly easy to manage by using insect protection, such as long-lasting fly sprays, topical medications and fly masks with ear protection. Severe cases may require oral anti-inflammatory treatment.

If your horse starts to display balance problems and/or is constantly shaking his/her head, definitely consult your vet as this may be an inner ear issue.

Our Queen Blondie

When I was having behaviour issues with one of my mares, okay Ms Foxy, I was advised to twist one of her ears when she danced and refused to stand quiet for the vet. Every instinct in my body screamed this was not the thing to do but, because this was advice from an experienced specialist of all things horsey, I went against my gut feeling. I twisted that ear when she started dancing away from the advances of the vet. Ohhhhhh...that became a big, big, big mistake.

The very second I twisted her left ear, my feet, in harmony with her front feet, were whipped into a violent upward motion that jolted my rotator cuff so abruptly I felt my arm was about to disconnected from my shoulder. My solid grip on her ear became a lot less solid and I found myself unceremoniously dumped in a heap on the ground staring straight up at the thrashing hooves of a very terrified mare.

She was tied to a tree and in her fight or flight response up was her only option. I could only cover my head with my arms preparing for the blow that I believed was about to come cracking down on me. But Ms Foxy deliberately twisted her thousand pound body away from me; ripping her right hind leg against the tree. The halter snapped setting her free to run like the devil was chasing her.

And run she did. No word of a lie, it took me two days to get near her again, a good week or more to get a halter on her and three years before I could touch her ears without her pulling away and giving me the stink-eye stare.

This was not Foxy's fault or problem. It was mine. I could have been seriously injured if not killed. Lucky for me Foxy did not respond in like kind. She was smarter and more considerate than I had been. She took a second injury to avoid hurting me. The sudden unexpected pain simply put her into an orbital flight mode.

Fox didn't want to hurt me; she simply wanted to escape the severe pain. A pain she now associated with the vet and worst of all, me. Oh... the problems I just created were years correcting. All because I followed advice that I did not feel as deeply in my spirit as I did in my mind, to be wise council.

I knew nothing about the ears. I had no idea the base of the pinna supported 10 auricular muscles with an even greater number of nerves supporting those muscles. But I know now. I also know twisting, squeezing or pulling on a horse's ear will and did cause sudden severe pain.

We all know for every action there is going to be a reaction. It's the reaction we need to anticipate and decide whether it's worth the action about to be taken. In this instance, for Foxy and I, nope it wasn't and I knew that. My need to please the experienced horse person was greater than my need to respect my horse.

I understand it's not uncommon for an experienced horse person to grab and twist the ear of a badly behaving horse in an effort to get him/her to submit to and figure out a standstill will decrease pain. I also understand it can be an extremely effective restraint. But, for me and mine, I will never again use that tactic as a restraint....so many other methods, with some homeopathic, may take a little more time and patience, but work just as effectively.

There are a great number of nerves in the base of the ear and there is a risk of damage that could result in permanent droopiness or floppiness. So never use a twitch on the ear. If the cartilage is damaged, the ear can become permanently disfigured and impair one of the first lines of defense of your horse. I'll probably stir the pot with this one, but for me, that is just plain and simple horse abuse.

Foxy is still not at ease around the vet. Forty-five minutes before the scheduled vet visit Foxy is given a small amount of her favourite sweetfeed laced with 60 mls of a homeopathic sedation called Equine Chill. Foxy has never exhibited any untoward behaviour or symptoms of distress post Equine Chill. For approximately 1 hour Ms Foxy will have a subdued awareness of the vet without the connection to pain. Slowly remove the fear. That's all good. All remain safe. Care is given and that works for me and Ms Foxy.

Chapter II

Horses make a landscape look beautiful..... Alice Walker

Facts about the Eyes

The horse has the largest eyes of any land mammal....well except maybe the moose. The visual abilities of your horse are directly related to his/her behaviour. Factor in that horses are, by nature, a flight animal.

When working with or training your horse the strengths and weaknesses of your horses visual abilities should always be taken into consideration. I started to realize this when I began to work with my one eyed Foxy and researched how to work with a horse with only one eye.

An awareness and understanding of your horse's eyes will help to discover and understand why he/she behaves in certain ways in various situations.

Horse's eyes are located on the side of their head giving them a wide range of vision of nearly 360 degrees with blind spots only immediately in front and immediately behind their bodies.

When looking straight ahead humans enjoy a clear field of vision. We have to turn our head from side to side to increase our peripheral field of vision.

Horses on the other hand have amazing peripheral vision but when staring straight ahead have two blind spots. One blind spot located directly in front of its nose extending out in a cone shape approximately four feet in front of the horse. The other blind spot behind the tail also extending out in a cone shape to about ten feet directly behind the tail.

Your horse uses both eyes separately which means they utilize monocular vision. Your horse can see and process different things happening on different sides of its body at the same time.

Your horse also has the ability to focus both eyes on a single object in front of it. Your horse will raise its head to increase his/her field of binocular vision and focus more acutely on things in the distance.

Your horse can't use monocular vision and binocular vision at the same time. Your horse switches the type of vision it is using by changing the position of its head to face the object.

I didn't realize that most horses don't walk backwards voluntarily because, in their world, what they can't see doesn't exist. I have a new appreciate and respect for the faith and trust I receive from my babies every time I ask one to simply step backward.

The trust between the horse and rider witnessed with equestrian jumping is in itself nothing short of a miracle. The horse will lose sight of the jumping obstacle when it is a few feet away and has to rely totally on the rider to signal it when to jump. That is the epitome of team work when the synergy between horse and rider is called to task.

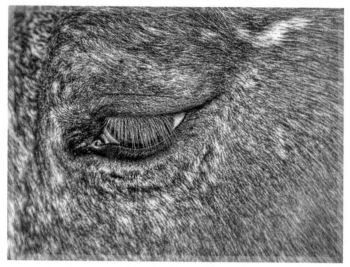

close up of Roxie's eye

Chapter III

**Bread may feed my body, but my horse
feeds my soul....**unknown

Digestion in the horse

For some, this section will be an informative refresher read. For the rest us, this will be information vital to understanding the process of digestion of our horse. A crash course in the anatomy and physiology of our horses is required to ensure normal delivery of the horse's most important creature comforts, food and water.

In spite of the strength, speed and stamina of the horse, their digestion systems are remarkably delicate. They are by diet herbivore specialists. Too much, too little or the wrong kind of foods can cause digestive upsets that can lead to illness or fatality.

Digestion in the horse is not the same as cattle and sheep. Technically, cows and sheep have one stomach as well, but that one stomach is divided into 4 very distinct compartments. Quite different from the horse and that is why people often say cows and sheep have 4 stomachs.

Horses traditionally had to graze little and often to maintain nutrient intake, usually more than 16 hours a day. They eat slowly and absorb nutrients continuously through the day and hence, became known as "slow feeders".

As with any living mammal, digestion starts in the mouth. Anything anyone digests has to start with putting the scrumptious in our mouth and munching down. Hmm...... try that without teeth; could be a painfully difficult challenge. Therefore this discussion on digestion will start at the very beginning, from the horse's mouth to your ear, so to speak.

<u>TEETH</u>

Just like humans, the horse will also have two sets of teeth but for horses the males have 44 teeth while female have 36-40 teeth. The majority of mares will have 36 teeth.

Male have canine teeth located between the incisors and the cheek teeth called the 'fighting teeth' because those boys will fight and bite to establish dominance of the herd.

Not to be confused with the "Wolfe teeth". The Wolfe teeth are premolars thought to be the equine version of wisdom teeth. The Wolfe teeth are often pulled/filed down to accommodate a bit.

Apparently 28% of mares will also develop canine teeth. Usually these mares are described as dominant but on occasion sometimes not. I've read you can leave them or take them out. But that would be a decision best made in consultation with your veterinarian along with the circumstance of both horse and rider.

At 2 to 3 years of age, a young horse will lose its milk teeth (baby teeth) and like you and I, get its one and only set of adult teeth. Except, unlike you and me, the teeth of an adult horse will continue to grow throughout most of its life. This creates specific patterns of tooth growth making it possible to estimate the age of the horse.

Horses spend 95% of their grazing time with their mouth and teeth close to the ground and thereby ingest a fair amount of grit. Grit continually grinds down the horse's teeth.

The continual grinding down by grit may not have the same effect if the horse is not eating from the ground on pasture grass. Therefore, tooth wear can be uneven or growth can exceed the amount of wear. Sometimes uneven edges can develop causing sores on the cheeks and tongue.

Yearly equine dentistry by a veterinarian is recommended to remove any excess growth or sharp edges that could form. The vet will use a metal rasp (big file) to "float the teeth". He will file down those rough edges. The filing doesn't hurt (no nerves there). Floating can reduce pain, mouth odor, problems with wearing a bit, eating and weight loss.

The length of the teeth can be used as measurement of age for younger horses but becomes less accurate on older horses 10 -14 years of age and older. The teeth of stabled horses can present the horse as younger while range horses can appear older because of the wear on the teeth.

That old saying "never look a gift horse in the mouth" dates back to a time in history when the vehicle of transportation for man was the horse. To be given a horse was considered a very generous gift. To inspect the teeth to determine its age and health was considered incredibly discourteous and offensive; actually very rude. Hence, "don't look a gift horse in the mouth" became the etiquette guideline to accepting a gift as is, with grace and appreciation.

SWALLOWING

Horses hold their food at the back of their mouth before swallowing. The mulched food becomes thoroughly mixed with saliva and is propelled down the esophagus (throat) by strong muscular contractions.

STOMACH

Food then travels to the horse's small one and only stomach that functions best if it is never quite full. A full stomach may be very satisfying to the rider, but very uncomfortable and even harmful for the horse.

The stomach valve on the horse only opens one way and therefore the horse **cannot** regurgitate. If something is consumed and disrupts the digestive system there is only one direction it can go, straight through to the back door and out.

In the stomach food is mixed with more acid and enzymes that help break the food down.

Food then travels into the small intestine.

SMALL INTESTINE

Food in the small intestine is broken down into basic components (the nutrients and energy that the horse requires) by more secretions from the intestine, liver and pancreas.

The food travels through the small intestine and enters the large intestine.

LARGE INTESTINE (Hindgut)

This where most of the water is extracted from the food and the fiber is broken down. The caecum (pronounced '*see come*') is located in a section of the large intestine which acts as a large fermentation vat where microorganisms break down feeds via the process of fermentation.

This process is relatively delicate as the bacteria population in the hindgut of the horse are designed to process fibrous sources of energy. The process of digestion can take up to 48 hours.

If a high starch diet is suddenly introduced, such as a high grain diet, the bacteria composition will change and an excess of heat, gas and acid will be produced. This can also, depending on how much and how often grain is fed, lead to the bacteria dying off and the release of endotoxins, which can increase the risk of laminitis, colic and acidosis.

From the large intestine feces travels to the rectum and is expelled through the anus and with graceful posturing is deposited on that freshly cleaned stall floor.

Constipation/colic can occur as a result of food impacting in the narrow bends within the intestinal system. Twisting or telescoping of the gut can occur causing extreme pain and in some instance death. Colic will be discussed in greater detail in another section of this book.

Put an ear or stethoscope to the side of the horse's belly. You should hear the melodic rumble and gurgling of a healthy functioning gut. Absolute music to your years that captivating awesome symphony of 'all is well in both our worlds' coming from a rumbling and gurgling tummy.

HORSE FURNACE

Literally and figuratively a 'right on' analogy when one considers two by-products of the digestive process are gas and heat. Usually gas passes harmlessly but the timing of such an event can be impeccable.

How many times have you been deep in thought while mindlessly brushing out the tail, when, without warning the SLF (Stealth-like Fart) strikes catching you off guard and unable to avoid the head fogging of a sudden warm blast of a pungent aroma wafting up both nostrils straight to the sinuses. A nose squinting and eye squeezing moment of true hilarity you wouldn't trade for anything. Makes your heart sing.

The heat generated by the digestive process is important for keeping the horse warm during frigid temperatures. Best way to keep a horse warm is to give free access to hay.

Chapter IV

Give a horse what he needs and he will
give you his heart..anonymous

The Essentials for Maintaining a Healthy Gut

All of these points have been discussed or about to be
discussed. This is an overview of the 'must haves' in order
to keep your horse healthy and happy. If this is what you
know, then you know a lot.

- Provide plenty of clean water
- Good quality hay and/or pasture
- Low NSC (non-structural carbohydrate) feed
- Plenty of exercise
- Regular de-worming program
- Regular dental care
- Regular foot care by farrier

Chapter V

The Consequence of an Unhealthy Cut

COLIC

Colic is a life threatening condition that is a result of a delicate digestive system out of balance and/or dehydration. Maintaining the requirements listed above for a healthy gut can have a great impact on eliminating this problem.

A horse does not vomit. Horses can suffer digestive distress from toxic plants, stress, bacteria (ie salmonella, parasites), blockage from overeating without sufficient water and swallowing foreign objects. All of which can result in colic. Colic is an indication of abdominal pain and is not a condition in itself. Colic symptoms include:

- Dull, listless or unusually irritated behaviour
- Kicking or biting at the sides (looking at the abdomen)

- Distended abdomen
- Getting up and down
- Violent rolling on the ground
- Constipation
- Reduced number of poops
- Decreased gut sounds
- Elevated pulse
- Sweating
- Refusal to eat or drink

If a horse is exhibiting colic symptoms call a veterinarian immediately. At all times personal safety is paramount. Remain calm, cool and controlled thereby decreasing the risk of increasing your horses already anxious, stressful state.

- In consultation with your vet, offer a warm soupy mixture of sweetfeed and bran. Giving bran to a horse under 4 years of age may not be recommended.
- Mix 1 cup of sweetfeed and 2 – 3 cups of bran with at least 2 – 3 gallons of warm water to make a warm soupy liquid that your horse can slurp
- If possible walk the horse continuously until gas/feces is passed and/or the vet arrives.

Chapter VI

A horse doesn't care how much you know, until
he knows how much you care...Pat Parelli

Understanding why horses don't vomit

It is physically impossible for a horse to vomit. If one considers the muscles of the horses lower esophageal valve are much stronger than in other animals making it nearly impossible to open the valve under backward pressure from the stomach.

Also the horse's esophagus joins the stomach at a much lower angle than many animals. When the stomach is distended it presses against the valve holding it even more tightly closed.

Also because the horse's stomach is located deep within the rib cage, it can't be squeezed by abdominal muscles.

It is suspected horses have a weak vomiting reflex because the neural pathways that control that activity in other animals is poorly developed in horses, if it exists at all.

We know the 'how' but the 'why' is unknown. One theory is when running at a full gallop the back and forth motion of their body cannot induce vomiting.

Another hypothesis is based on the fact horses are built to graze; take in very small portions at a time as they feed throughout the day and are fairly fussy about the plants they ingest.

Therefore, it's possible they never needed to vomit because they would rarely consume toxic doses of any vegetation. If they did, it would be a very small amount. Horses are very selective of the plants they will eat and those they won't. They are definitely not goats.

Although there have been reported incidents of horse's vomiting, it is more feasible these cases were a matter of regurgitation from a blocked esophagus and not from the stomach.

Vomiting is a reflex muscular action that expels material under great pressure while regurgitation is passive. If the esophageal muscles go flaccid, ingested food held in the back of the mouth or in the throat may regurgitate as ooze from the nose and mouth.

Chapter VII

Horseback riding is life, the rest is just details....unknown

Food

Through-out history man has employed food as a universal language. For centuries food has been used as an ally to bridge differences and misunderstandings; as a balm to sooth pain and suffering; and as a foundation for reward and celebration.

The unspoken world of the horse is no different. When food is offered to the horse, a bridge of trust and respect begins to link us to a century's old existence founded in respectful civility and infinite wisdom. The very world we seek is right in front of us. Food is the key and anyone can enter.

As it is for the human dietary needs, the same six general classes of nutrients are required in the horse's dietary needs.

- Water
- Carbohydrates
- Protein
- Fats
- Minerals
- Vitamins

Now that the mechanics of digestion have been discussed, it's time to examine the food used in the horse's digestion system and recognize the impact of "you are what you eat" has on our big four legged family members.

As already discussed, the horse's digestive system is geared toward a slow, continual intake of grass, hay and other types of forage. Horses require an abundance of energy and most of this energy comes from carbohydrates found in fiber in the hay and/or other types of forage.

Carbohydrates, protein and fiber are the three macro-nutrients contained in the vegetation consumed by the horse.

There is so much information on carbohydrates with some easier to understand and interpret than others; with other information so hard to understand and so difficult to interpret. It was daunting sorting through these macro-nutrients, most particularly carbohydrates.

The chemical breakdown of carbohydrates into starch and sugars with some good and some bad and yet all relative, compounded with the issues of the digestive process, very quickly began to boggle the brain bucket never mind the feed bucket. Add to the mixture the scientific jargon and you just know confusion and frustration began to invade the thought processes and cloud the grey cells.

The topic of carbohydrates for horses has become such a hot topic among horse people. The internet and horse magazine's are full of articles, editorials and commentaries addressing the issues of healthy feeding of our horses and in particular the good and bad of carbohydrates.

Chapter VIII

A horse is worth more than riches.....Spanish Proverb

Nutrients

As identified earlier there are six general classes of nutrients essential to life and they are water, carbohydrates, protein, fats, vitamins and minerals. They will be discussed individually starting at the beginning with the wonders of water through to the must of minerals.

1. Water

Water is the most important nutrient, bar none. Without water almost all of your horse's systems cease to function. Water aids in the maintenance of the horse's body temperature; it lubricates the joints and helps cushion the central nervous system. It is involved in both sight and hearing.

Water aids in digestion; acts as a solvent for toxins and helps eliminate them through urine and sweat. Water is necessary to help maintain an elastic skin tone. Water is very important.

Horses quickly become dehydrated without sufficient water. They can survive without food for up to three weeks but they can only survive without water for a maximum of five to six days.

Dehydration can also occur with excessive water loss through sweating because of heat and humidity and stressful exercise. A horse's need for water can increase 3 to 4 times with work/exercise during hot weather temperatures.

Horses with diarrhea or scours also become dehydrated quite rapidly, and the water loss in this case makes thermo-regulation difficult and often contributes to fever.

Incidence of impaction colic increases from December to March often because water supply is decreased because of freezing of natural sources and plumbing systems.

Horses are prone to impaction colic any time they are fed hay or roughage cubes and face a rapid decrease in water availability and consumption. Horses grazing on fresh, juicy pasture can extract much of their water needs from their grass intake.

Mares in foal or lactating have increased needs for water. Foals satisfy most of their liquid requirements by nursing; most begin to drink water at one to two weeks. It's a habit that begins early and lasts a lifetime.

To ensure your horse never experiences dehydration, make sure he/she always has access to clean, fresh water, regardless of the weather. No matter what you've been told, eating snow and/or munching on ice chips will not cut it.

Water is the ultimate essential element of life and dehydration is a situated best prevented.

2. Carbohydrates

Carbohydrates are an essential component of every horse's diet. They are found in almost all the food the horse eats, including forages, grains, and by-products of forage and grain. Carbohydrates are a component of food that supplies energy (calories) to the body.

The confusion for me began with the terms of carbohydrates, starches, sugars, non-structural carbohydrates (NSC), non-fibrous carbohydrates (NFC) and structural carbohydrates; all very intimidating when it came to understanding just what these nutrients meant to the equine diet and how much our horses need or don't need to ensure optimal health and well being.

The information researched was often confusing, perplexing and baffling not to mention daunting. So many times I found myself feeling so frustrated looking for the dunce cap instead of the baseball cap. It 'twas a challenge, but when you have horses you are always up for the challenge.... correct?

This was a very complex, confusing and in the language of biology, a challenging topic to reduce to its most common denominator in layman's language.

Trying to remember on Friday, 'what did I do on Monday?' is a challenge some days, never mind trying to recall the language of biology from long, long, long ago high school days.

Trying to remember high school biology would have required a mini refresher course except I was saved by the very smart folks that encompass my circle of life. So to keep it simple, I simply went brain picking. Oh and I do confess….I also dug out an old biology book from my daughter's not so long ago high school days.

I am not going to talk about carbohydrates on a molecular biological level. But it is important to distinguish between the health-robbing effects of simple sugars and the health-giving properties of complex carbohydrates.

Carbohydrates are an energy source in food that comes from starch, sugar and cellulose. Carbohydrates also provide vitamins, minerals, antioxidants and fiber in the diet.

There are two types of carbohydrates, those in their natural food form comprise of a long chain of carbohydrates (three or more) linked together and referred to as "complex" and those that are smaller pieces (one or two sugars) and referred to as "simple".

Complex carbohydrates are foods which contain vitamins, minerals and antioxidants. Complex carbohydrates cause an increased and faster blood sugar elevation. They are produced within the plant by the plant as a means to store energy and therefore contain readily available energy.

Starches are composed of long chains of glucose (strings of sugars) linked together. Most starches are broken down into glucose in the small intestine by the action of enzymes, primarily amylase.

Horses produce less amylase than other animals, therefore limited in their ability to digest large quantities of starch but horses can digest smaller quantities very efficiently and very effectively!

Simple carbohydrates (sugar) are easily digested and rapidly absorbed causing a spike in blood sugar and quick boost in energy. Simple carbohydrates cause more and faster blood sugar elevation than complex carbohydrates.

Simple carbohydrates are broken down by enzymes (primarily amylase) and absorbed from the small intestine into the blood stream as glucose. This glucose is stored as glycogen in the muscles and in the liver. A sedentary life style together with time creates the fatty patties and hunky chunkies.

Carbohydrates provide energy. The source of the carbohydrate, along with the method of digestion, always determines the amount of energy that is going to be available for the horse.

The base unit of a carbohydrate is the monosaccharide (mono = one; saccharide = sugar). How this basic unit connects to form different carbohydrates determines the site of digestion and the nutritional value received.

The most common monosaccharide is glucose. Glucose is the sugar that circulates in the blood and is the primary source of energy for cells. Monosaccharides by themselves are very low in plant foods that are consumed by the horse but are found in various quantities in fruits, berries vegetables and honey.

The importance of monosaccharides is how they link together to form more complex saccharides (natural sugar) in plants that provide a fuel source for the horse.

Carbohydrates divided into two general categories known as structural and nonstructural carbohydrates. We have looked at the types of carbohydrates. Know we need to look at what type of carbohydrate fits into what category of carbohydrate. We then need to know what carbohydrate is good and which is maybe, not so good and why.

General Categories of Carbohydrates

Structural carbohydrates (complex carbohydrates) are also identifed as fiber and are digested by microorganisms throughout the gut but primarily the hindgut. If you are confused about fiber, you are not alone. Dietary fiber is a misunderstood nutrient. Dietary fibers are found naturally in plants.

Dietary fiber is part of a plant that does not breakdown in the stomachs. Instead passes directly through to the hindgut.

Two main types of fiber are soluble and insoluble. Both types of fiber passe through the digestive system undigested.

Soluble fiber:

- Dissolves in water
- Attracts water and forms a gel (creates feeling of fullness; controls weight)
- Slower stomach emptying; beneficial effect on insulin sensitivity
- Helps lower LDL (that bad cholesterol); interferes with absorption of dietary cholesterol

Foods high in Soluble fibre: oatmeal, oat cereal, lentils, apples, oranges, pears, oat bran, strawberries, nuts, flaxseeds, beans, dried peas, blueberries, psyllium, cucumbers, celery, and carrots. All digestible by the owner/rider but not all are digestible by the horse.

Insoluble fiber:

- Have a laxative effect
- Add bulk to the diet preventing constipation
- Doesn't dissolve in water; passes through gastrointestinal tract relatively intact
- Will speed up the passage of food and waste through gut

Foods high in insoluble fibre: whole wheat, whole grains, wheat bran, corn bran, seeds, nuts, barley, couscous, brown rice, bulgur, zucchini, celery broccoli, cabbage, onions, tomatoes, carrots, cucumbers, green beans, dark leafy vegetables, raisins, grapes, fruit and root vegetable skins. Again, all digestible by the owner/rider but not all are digestible by the horse. Those good for your horse and those not so good for your horse are identified and discussed in another section. Just keep reading.

Third type of fiber is also known as resistant starch. Produced by plants as a means to store energy and therefore contain readily available energy. It is known as the third type of fiber because it has some of the benefits of soluble and insoluble fiber. Resistant starch is considered both a dietary fiber and a functional fiber. It is a type of starch that "escapes" or "resists" digestion in the small intestine and cannot be broken down easily by enzymes (amylase) in the small intestine and that's all good!

Resistant starch (the third type of fiber) passes through the small intestine and into the large intestine (colon) without being absorbed by the body and must be fermented in the caecum of the large intestine to release the energy; does not raise blood sugar levels. And that too is all good.

The energy available in resistant starch fiber is less immediately available requiring release thru fermentation.

Resistant starch can be found naturally in whole grains, fruits, and legumes, including: oats, rye, wheat (whole grain breads), pearl barley, semolina, corn, linseed for flax oil, lentils, baked beans, navy beans, brown rice and raw slightly green bananas and plantains.

Feed that is high in fiber is low in NSC (non structural carbohydrates) and therefore low in energy. An example would be grass hay which is high in fiber and low in NSC and energy. While corn, on the other hand is very low in fiber and high in NSC and energy.

Beet pulp and soy hull are high in fiber and low in starch and do not contain the high starch contained in corn and barley.

The starch in oats is more digestible by the horse than the starch in corn. Also, as the starch content of a diet increases, meal size and frequency should decrease.

Sugars provide no nutrition aside from energy; hence they are often referred to as empty calories.

The optimal diet for your horse will be composed mostly of forage in which fiber or complex carbohydrates will comprise most your horse's carbohydrate intake. Forages also provide your horse with some simple carbohydrates as well, such as starch and sugar.

If high amounts of energy are required then the grains in your horses diet will be source of energy required.

Nonstructural carbohydrates (NSC)

Non-Structural Carbohydrates (NSC), now this is important stuff, are also identified as starches and sugars. NSC's are digested by enzymes and absorbed in the foregut (small intestine).

NSC consists of **both** simple carbohydrates (**sugar**) and complex carbohydrates (**starch**). An important group of nutrients for horses because they create high amounts of energy.

NSC are broken down by amylase into glucose and absorbed from the small intestine into the blood stream. They are stored as glycogen in the muscle and in the liver. Too much NSC creates spikes in blood glucose levels.

NSC not absorbed in the small intestine and can be problematic in the caecum and large intestine causing hindgut acidosis, colic, laminitis and altered behavior.

High NSC index in horses is equal to elevated glycemic index in humans; in humans known as Type 2 diabetes; in horses known as insulin resistance.

Low carb diet for the horse translates into a low NSC diet. The accepted safe NSC level in feeds is 12%. Levels >12% can be fed when work level increases.

Fibre is the material of the plant cell wall that gives plants its rigidness. Fibre is the base of the horse diet. Horses evolved on a high fibre diet comprising of medium to low quality pastures. The horse's digestive tract has evolved to cater for this type of diet.

Average Sugar, Starch, Non-Structural Carbohydrate (NSC) Values of Selected Feedstuffs*

Feedstuff	Sugar	Starch	NSC
Oat Hay	16.0%	6.3%	22.1%
Barley Hay	14.9%	5.8%	20.4%
Alfalfa Hay	8.9%	2.5%	11.3%
Bermudagrass Hay	7.5%	6.1%	13.6%
Grass Hay	1.1%	2.9%	13.8%
Alfalfa Pellets	7.2%	2.3%	9.3%
Alfalfa Cubes	8.3%	2.0%	10.2%
Grass Pasture	10.3%	3.4%	12.1%
Rice Bran	6.2%	17.7%	21.2%
Oats	4.8%	44.4%	54.1%
Corn	3.7%	70.3%	73.3%
Barley	6.0%	53.7%	61.7%
Beet Pulp	10.7%	1.4%	12.3%
Wheat Bran	8.3%	2.8%	31.1%
Soybean Hulls	4.3%	1.9%	6.3%
Wheat Middlings	10.1%	26.2%	32.0%
Soybean Meal	14.3%	2.1%	16.2%

*Values were compiled by the Equi-Analytical Laboratories, Ithaca, NY.

3. Protein

Protein is required to build tissue in all living things, including horses. Protein in a horse's diet serves the same purpose it does in a human's diet. It's needed to build tissue for strong bones and muscles; for the growth and repair of tissues; for good general health and energy; with growth and reproduction being the most critical time periods.

To ensure a proper amount of protein in equine diets, begin with quality forage and then supplement as needed with a balanced concentrate designed for the type of horse you are feeding.

Protein is found in plant life contained in hay/forage. Also rich in protein are vegetables, grains and legumes

Proteins are formed by amino acids. Amino acids are defined as any of a large number of compounds found in living cells that contain carbon, oxygen, hydrogen and nitrogen that join together to form protein.

Protein is also made up of different amino acids; some synthesized within the horses body; some are not (aka <u>essential</u> amino acids) and must be supplied in feeds.

The protein consumed by the average horse should be in the realm of that available from the start in the mare's milk – 12% protein.

Hay (the mainstay of your horse's diet)

Majority of protein in the horse's diet comes from hay. Hay falls into one of two categories...grasses or legumes. Horse hay is often a mixture of the two depending on which part of the country you live.

Nutritional value and palatability depends on a number of factors, such as:

- plant species and level of plant maturity at harvest
- soil conditions and fertility
- weed content and growing conditions (weather, insects, disease etc)
- curing and harvesting conditions
- moisture content
- length and method of storage

The majority of protein in the diet comes from hay. Increased protein levels are not responsible for a "hot" horse. Protein is a very inefficient source of energy. Protein's main use in a mature horse is the re-building of muscle and other body cells.

Legume Hay

Alfalfa and clover are examples of legumes with alfalfa the more common; clover can be a component of mixed hay. Legume hay is higher in protein, energy, calcium and Vitamin A than grass hay and it can be fed as part of the ration for young, growing horses, lactating mares and performance athletes.

Lower quality hay (early cutting; harvested in a late stage of plant maturity; alfalfa grass mix hay) delivers alfalfa's dietary benefits minus excess nutrients that may predispose younger horses to problems such as developmental bone disease and epiphysitis.

In council with your veterinarian, and in order to maintain the calcium/phosphorous ratio balance, you may need to enhance lower quality legume hay with a palatable high phosphorus supplement; especially when feeding young, growing horses. Never give nutrient supplements without first consulting with your veterinarian.

Your horse will likely drink more water when fed legume hay and as well, your horse's stall will be wetter and require more care to keep it clean, dry and ammonia-free.

Grass Hay

Grass hay is lower in protein and energy but higher in fiber than legume hay. Grass hay is the best choice for many adult horses. It satisfies your horse's appetite while providing necessary roughage without excess calories and protein.

Good quality grass hay meets most of adult horse's basic nutritional needs. Mature horses require 10% - 12% crude protein in their diet and this goal is obtained with good quality grass hay.

Fortified grain concentrate can supplement the feed ration, increasing its energy, protein, vitamin and mineral content. Common varieties of grass hay include timothy, orchard, brome, fescue, prairie or wild native, oat, Bermuda.

the three runners, Chance, Foxy and Catman

Signs and Symptoms of decreased protein in horse's diet include:

- lose skin condition
- may become unusually lethargic (not himself)
- should consider if your Ferrier advises of a problem with his/her hooves
- can also predispose your horse to hypothyroidism and tying up.

Signs and Symptoms of increased protein in horse's diet include:

- Increased urination; if your horse is known to urinate more often than other horses
- a strong ammonia odor
- can also predispose your horse to hypothyroidism, trying up, and arthritis

Recommended Total daily protein percentages of protein intake:

- Foal: 16-18%
- Weanlings: 14-16%
- Yearlings: 12-14%
- Mature horses: 10-12%
- Lactating mares: 12-14%

<u>Beet Pulp</u> – hay supplement

Beet pulp is the by-product resulting from the extraction of simple sugars in the manufacture of table sugar. The remaining pulp has little or no sucrose (table sugar) left in it. Manufacturer adds molasses that equates to the sugar content of a few apples.

Beet pulp NSC (non structural carbohydrate) content is low at 12%. Adding slightly more water to beet pulp and draining excess fluid (containing sugar from added molasses) reduces the NSC level even lower. It's actually a great feed for horses that need to put on weight and those who require feed that doesn't make a horse's blood sugar spike and dip.

In all that I have read, the jury is out on whether to serve dry or soaked. Those on the soak side will cite the increased probability of choking as any dry feed can cause choking; especially if the horse does not have free access to water or if the horse has other risk factors such as it seems to inhale its food.

It is believed that choke related to beet pulp is linked to the particle size and the horse's aggressive feeding behaviour rather than the actual feed itself.

Some horse owners are concerned that dry beet pulp will absorb water and swell in the horse's stomach creating digestion issues as impaction or colic. However, a properly hydrated horse usually produces enough saliva to moisten any feedstuff properly, including beet pulp.

Soaking the beet pulp as a means to prevent any choking issues is a good reason to soak the beet pulp but there are other good reasons as well. It will make the feed easier to chew particularly for older horses with dental issues. Soaking may improve the taste and regardless makes an excellent way to disguise those medications not taken willingly.

Horses will normally drink enough water to stay hydrated. But, during the winter months horses tend to drink less water than they need. Feeding soaked beet pulp will count as increasing the fluid intake.

Some dry beet pulp has been fed in amounts up to 45% of total diet with no instances of choke or other adverse reactions. My crew prefer soaked. Their preference becomes my command, so soaked it is. Beet pulp is only on their winter menu. Summer months they are on grass with access to hay and fresh water year round.

Soak beet pulp with cool or warm water and never use hot as this cooks the beet pulp and nutrients are lost.

Beet pulp can stretch your hay supply and encourage weight gain on your "hard keeper'. Helps horses with dental problems wherein chewing hay is difficult; assists older horses that have a hard time digesting other types of roughage (hay).

Beet pulp is a relatively inexpensive readily available feed that provides a consistent, cost effective forage alternative to extending your hay supply. Keep in mind, incorporating beet pulp into your horses feeding program does not provide balanced mineral and vitamin intake and must be provided by other ingredients in your horse's total diet.

Definitions for an easy understanding of fiber and protein intake:

- Forage - a feed with fiber content higher than 18% crude fiber
- Energy feed – a feed with less than 18% crude fiber and less than 20% crude protein
- Protein supplement – a feed with less than 18% crude fiber and higher than 20% crude protein
- Beet pulp – a feed with 18% crude fiber and 10% crude protein; sits on the edge between forage and energy food; most nutritionists utilize beet pulp as forage

Beet pulp information obtained from research conducted at several universities:

- Debra J Hagstrom, M.S. Equine Extension Specialist, University of Illinois)

- Tina Kemper, DVM, Diplomate ACVIM, of San Luis Rey Equine Hospital in Bonsall, Calif.
- Dr. Frederick Harper, extension horse specialist at the University of Tennessee's Animal Science Department,
- Anne Rodiek, Department of Animal Sciences and Agricultural Education, California State University, Fresno, California

A little food for thought. Carnivore meat has protein because they eat animals that eat plants. That's why carnivores are not known to normally hunt and eat other carnivores. In fact carnivores are known to first eat the intestines of their kill because that's where the nutrients are located. Yes the first thing eaten are the intestines containing the plants the animal ate.

Protein given to our horses from animal by-products would become a breeding ground for bacteria causing severe digestive problems for horses. Horses like all vegans simple cut to the chase and go straight to the protein source.... plants!

4. Lipids (Fat and Oil)

Hundreds of years ago when horse traders wanted a horse to gain weight and develop a slick hair coat they added oil to the diet. Current literature recognizes grain could be replaced with oils up to a level of 10 – 15% in the diet.

Since the 1980's feeding fat to horses has become more popular and feed stores now offer a selection of fat added feeds. The digestive system of the horse can handle fats quite well.

Oils have always been present in a horse's diet as grasses are typically 2 – 3% oil and therefore horses present as well equipped to digest oils.

The term "seed oil" is now used to describe oils produced from crops that have been industrialised, e.g. canola and soy which are usually genetically modified.

Lipids are an important part of the horse's body. Lipids consist of the majority of cell walls, transport fat-soluble vitamins to their required destinations and are integral in many other body functions.

Lipid digestion occurs primarily in the small intestine, via the production and release of digestive enzymes and bile salts. As the horse does not possess a gall bladder, bile salts are continually released into the intestine from the liver.

The type of fats (lipids) fed to horses are known as triglycerides, consisting of three fatty acid molecules attached to a glycerol molecule. The chemistry of the fatty acid molecules determines if the fat is saturated or unsaturated oil. Triglycerides are the most common lipid found in the horse's body.

Saturated Fats

Saturated fatty Acids (SFA) contain no double bonds in the fatty acid chains and are solids at room temperature.

Saturated fats (SFA) are required for proper digestive function, growth and a host of other processes. They are an essential component of every single cell in both our bodies and that of our horse.

At the core of all fatty acids is a chain of carbon atoms. Fatty acids come in many lengths with many names. All saturated fats are essentially straight and the molecules can be packed tightly together. This makes them relatively dense and solid at room temperature.

A common example of saturated fat is lard or tallow (animal fat) and coconut oil (plant fat).

Coconut oil is considered one of Mother Nature's near perfect food right along with honey. Both nature's best.

Coconut oil is a **medium** chain fatty acid aka MCFA. It is a palatable source of saturated fatty acids. It is also a source of omega 6. MCFAs are easier to digest, absorb and utilise for energy than the longer chain fatty acids of Omega 6 found in vegetable oil seeds.

The key benefits of coconut oil are it's easier to digest, absorb and utilize than vegetable oils. It provides a ready source of energy. It increases performance benefits by lowering lactate and ammonia levels with higher free fatty acids.

Coconut is considered a cool feed because there is no fermentation and heat production associated with digestion of this saturated fat. It also increases stamina and strengthens the immune system.

Coconut does have anti-inflammatory and fever-reducing abilities along with antifungal, antiviral and antibacterial properties. It contains vitamin E, Vitamin K and Omega-6 (medium chain). It is used in traditional medicine to treat skin infections, upset stomach, wounds, bronchitis and coughs. As a saturated fat, coconut oil will stay fresh for a long time.

Unsaturated Fat (oil)

Unsaturated fat (oil) contains double bonds and are liquid at room temperature. The location of the double bond within the fatty acid is also used to identify omega 3 and omega 6 fatty acids.

Fats and oils consist of chains of carbon atoms connected together in assorted ways with two oxygen atoms at one end forming an organic acid and therefore these are called fatty acids

Fatty acids are a component of all cell membranes. Some fatty acids are manufactured by the micro-organisms of the natural flora of the gut. Other fatty acids cannot be manufactured by the body and must come from the diet. Fatty acids that must come from food sources are referred to as 'essential fatty acids' as they are essential for robust health and can only be provided in the diet.

As this is not meant to be a chemistry lesson, the concentration will be on essential fatty acids obtained from food sources.

Lipids are divided into two classes:

- **Fats** – saturated fats - derived from animals and solid at room temperature
- **Oils** - unsaturated fats - derived from plants and liquid at room temperature

Exceptions: (what would life be without the exceptions!)

- **Fish oil** - derived from animal and liquid at room temperature
- **Coconut oil** - derived from plants and solid at room temperature

Fats derived from animal sources are not going to be discussed because our horses are herbivores of the first order and for centuries the object of all predators. Examples of oils fed to horses include corn oil, soybean oil, canola oil and coconut oil.

Only fats obtained from plants essential to the well being of our horses will be the focus of this discussion.

Fats have 3 essential functions in the diet/metabolism of our horses. Fats are necessary for the absorption of fat soluble vitamins A, D, E and K from the gut.

Essential fatty acids, the omega-3 and omega-6, are required for the synthesis of some of the chemicals required by the body for normal function. They are a concentrated source of energy.

Considering that horses have evolved as a grazing animal whereby natural foodstuffs are very low in fats, horses can still tolerate relatively high concentrations in the diet. Good thing because fat supplement diets can be beneficial in several equine disease conditions.

While we humans struggle to keep our diets as low-fat as possible, fat has a totally different focus when it comes to our horses. In recent years it has been recognized that raising fat levels in the athletic horse's diet has an ever increasing value as to overall health and performance especially if that fat is based in coconut oil.

Carbohydrates have long been considered the first choice and 'natural' energy source for performance horses. Beyond adding a dash or two of corn oil to feed for a shiny coat, fat was never considered as having many advantages including that of a valuable energy source. But over the past couple of decades research into the value of fat as an energy source has proved its worth and value in this area.

A standard grain-plus-forage diet provides approximately a 2% to 3.5% fat content to our horses' diet. But it has been discovered a high-fat diet energy production is almost 2 ½ times that of NSC sugar and starch (found in grains such as oats, corn or barley).

So, if you want to cut down on overall feed intake as well as decrease the assault of a sugar rush, supplementing fat in your horse's diet is an excellent way to accomplish that.

It has also been shown that a fat supplemented diet has no effect on the pH of the cecum because fat presents as being absorbed almost exclusively in the small intestine. Therefore any detrimental effect on the flora inhabiting the large intestines is eliminated. In contrast, a high-carbohydrate presents as a high risk to alter the natural flora in the hindgut as it is absorbed in the large intestine.

In spite of the fact our horses do not have a gallbladder, they can metabolize fats very well. The horse's liver seems to take over that function with no fat digestion problems any research has been able to identify.

It has also been discovered that fat-supplemented diets decrease the amount of energy used for heat production in the horse's body during times of required athletic performance. This decreases the horse's heat load and increases the amount of energy available for physical activity.

It also decreases the loss of fluid through the insensible losses of sweating that occurs with increased heat production during times of increased physical activity regardless of the existing temperature or how skinny or plump your high performance horse may be. It becomes a bonus for high performance horses involved in high-performance sports such as three-day eventing, racing, polo, endurance racing, cutting etc.

So in summary, horses on high fat diets can perform longer without fatigue, incur fewer injuries and maintain body weight with less grain intake, while maximizing forage intake. Adding fat to a horse's diet allows safe weight gain while reducing the chance of colic or founder, it may also allow lactating mares to breed back more readily. Products of horse feed using coconut oil would be among the best as coconut, along with honey, is considered to be one of Mother Nature's near perfect foods.

Mono-unsaturated fatty acids (MUFA)

Mono-unsaturated fatty acids (MUFA) are fatty acids that are missing one hydrogen pair on their chain. They are associated with lowering LDL (low density lipids) cholesterol (the not so good guy), total cholesterol and at the same time increasing the production of the "good guy" HDL (high density lipids) cholesterol. These fats are usually liquid at room temperature. Eat in moderation and use in balance with saturated fats.

Mono-unsaturated fats help to reduce bad cholesterol levels and lower risk of heart disease for the both the horse and especially the rider. They provide nutrients to develop and maintain body cells. They are also typically high in Vitamin E an antioxidant vitamin.

Foods high in mono-unsaturated fats include sunflower oil, canola oil, olive oil, peanut oil, hazel nuts, macadamia nuts and avocados, peanut butter and many nuts and seeds.

These food substances are not necessary conducive to equine consumption but definitely all good for the rider. Having said that, I have dedicated a whole section in this book to the foods we can share with our horse and those we can't. But, the creature comfort of our horses is also relative and directly linked to the health and welfare of their owners/ riders as both need to be at the top of their game when working together.

Poly-unsaturated Fatty Acids (PUFA)

Polyunsaturated fatty acids (PUFA)= two or more double bonds classified into two biologically important subgroups of omega-3 and omega-6.

Omega-3 – essential fatty acid found only in plants.

Omega-3's play a crucial role in normal growth and develop and in particular the functioning of the brain. Omega-3's are highly concentrated in the brain and are important for cognitive (brain memory and performance) and behaviour. The omega-3's also reduce inflammation and thereby lower chronic disease as well.

As herbivores and nomadic grazers, horses are naturally adapted to a diet rich in omega-3 fatty acids as compared to omega-6 fatty acids. And this I did not know; the fat found in forages, particularly fresh pasture, is naturally high in omega-3's whereas oils from grains and seeds tend to be higher in omega-6.

Depending on the maturity of the grass, the oils in fresh grass will be between 3% and 5% and that oil will contain 40% to 55% Omega 3's......Mother Nature is so good in her garden.

Not all the foods listed rich in omega-3 are palatable to our horses but, because the wellbeing of the rider is also an important factor in the creature comfort of horses, I've taken the liberty of listing all plant foods rich in Omega-3.

In another chapter I do discuss those foods good for our horses and those not so good....in the mean time savor the fact wine is rich in the essential fatty acid omega-3. After a long hard day a nightcap glass of wine can always be touted as just topping up one's omega-3's and boosting one's cognitive abilities.

Foods rich in omega-3's are whole grains, flax, hemp, canola, walnut, pumpkin seeds, soybeans (tofu) dark green veggies (kale, collards, chard, parsley, seaweed), cereal grasses (wheat, barley grasses), fresh fruit and vegetables, fish (algae and krill), olive oil, garlic and moderate wine consumption.

Fish store Omega-3 fats from the algae they consume. Fish themselves do not produce omega-3 fatty acids. They get it from the plant life they ingest. Plants are the essence of life for all mammal and marine life....no exceptions!

Omega-6 – essential fatty acid found only in plants. Omega-6 is needed by the body as it plays a vital role in the development and operation of many essential substances such as vitamins and minerals and physiological functions.

The function of Omega-6 is multi-faceted. Omega-6 is used in cell membranes to create flexibility and permeability. It promotes normal growth and development and it stimulates skin and hair growth.

Omega-6 also plays a crucial role in brain function. It also maintains bone health and regulates metabolism. It also plays a major role in the maintenance of the reproductive system. Where omega-3 reduces inflammation, omega-6 stimulates the inflammatory response when the body is subjected to any assault by a bacterial or viral invasion.

Foods rich in omega 6 fatty acids are sunflower, safflower, soybeans, hemp seeds, walnuts, pumpkin seeds, sesame seeds, fax seeds and most grains, wheat germ, walnut and sesame oils (cooking/salad), margarine (hydrogenated), mayonnaise dressing, olive oil, turkey and chicken, almonds (grounded), walnut (chopped), peanut butter, soybeans

Spoonful of food for thought and totally off topic, just something that struck me....without plant life there would be no life because the body of humans and animals cannot synthesize essential fatty acids, only plants can do that. Next to us, our horse's best friend is the bumble bee.....without pollination there would be no plant life.......

While I'm on the road of off topic thought I would share a little more information. Saturated fat and cholesterol have long been considered health hoodlums lurking in our food just to cause problems. This is simply not true. Mother Nature didn't put saturated fat in vegetables, mother's milk, and other foods just for the fun of it. Everything in our universe has order and purpose and never more clearly demonstrated than in the world of our horses.

Cholesterol is important to the basic operations of life. Without it, every cell would become dead masses of fat and protein. The membrane of our cells preferentially chooses saturated and mono-unsaturated fat for incorporation into its structure.

Cholesterol made from saturated fat by the liver and brain is the material used to build healthy cells. It is the "oxidized" or damaged cholesterol that finds its way inside artery walls and creates an inflammatory response.

Oxidized cholesterol is created when heated oil mixes with oxygen releasing free radicals. Coconut Oil when heated does not mix with oxygen and therefore does not release free radicals creating oxidize cholesterol. Olive oil is high in mono-unsaturated fats which are reported to be stable when heated.

Just a tidbit of information directly more at the rider than the horse, it is considered the normal ratio of omega 3 and omega 6 in a normal health diet should be approximately 1:1 to 1:4.

Every disease is considered to be the result of inflammatory response and scientists are now researching and questioning the imbalance of omega 3 and omega 6 consumption as the possible root evil for the increases in chronic diseases such as arthritis, lupus, etc. It is considered the normal ratio should be 1:1 to 1:4. Because of the high use of both mayonnaise (created with omega 6 rich oils) and the fast foods prepared with omega 6 rich oils, the ratio has become unbalanced.

It is now thought, in our world of instant everything, the ratio of omega 3: omega 6 is now greater than 1:16. Omega

3 acts as the brake pedal for the inflammatory response while omega 6 is the gas pedal. Consequently, we are now being encouraged to take omega 3 supplements to correct this imbalance.

5. Minerals

Minerals are inorganic compounds needed as components of body tissue and as facilitators of various body processes. The two minerals of largest requirements are calcium and phosphorus.

Minerals can be divided into two broad classifications:

Macro-minerals are required in large amounts in the diet. Calcium, phosphorus, magnesium, potassium, sodium, chlorine and sulfur are macro-minerals.

Macro-minerals are vital to the development of the skeleton, muscle contraction, acid-base balance and to the activity of the nervous system, hoof and hair growth.

Micro-minerals are only required in small amounts in the diet. Copper, iodine, iron, manganese, selenium and zinc are micro-minerals.

Micro-minerals are vital to chemical reactions that help to metabolize nutrients. They maintain connective tissue and joint tissue. Micro-minerals aid in oxygen transport to muscles and as well perform as antioxidants.

6. Vitamins

Vitamins are organic compounds needed in trace amounts that regulate a multitude of bodily functions. There are two general classes of vitamins: fat soluble and water soluble.

Fat-soluble Vitamins

Fat-soluble vitamins are absorbed with fat. Fat-soluble vitamins are A, D, and E. Fat-soluble vitamins are important for vision, calcium absorption and regulation.

They are also the primary antioxidant within the body protecting cells and muscle function. Fat-soluble vitamins are stored in the fat deposits of the body. They can accumulate if overfed creating a potential for toxicity.

Water-soluble vitamins are as one would suspect absorbed by water. Thiamin, riboflavin, niacin, biotin, folic acid (the B vitamins) and Vitamin C are critical in metabolism, growth and energy generation. B-vitamins are manufactured by healthy bacteria in our horse's digestive system.

Excess intake of fat-soluble vitamins A and D for your horse can be detrimental since fats, and the substances soluble in them, are poorly excreted from the body. Excessive intake of water-soluble vitamins is rarely detrimental as water-soluble substances are readily excreted from the body with urination.

In summary, feeding a horse a properly balanced diet is not hard if we remember that the small things (vitamins and minerals) are also very important.

Although it is suggested horses lack the rough tongue of cattle to adequately use salt and mineral blocks, I have them readily available. But a very experienced horsewoman advised me, on very hot days and after sweaty strenuous activity, she adds 1-2 tbsp of granulated salt in the daily feed. Remember sodium is a mineral required for muscle contraction and that includes heart muscle.

They know when they need to use the salt and mineral blocks and I have not witnessed any difficulty on their part and I replace them on a regular basis.

Commercially prepared horse feeds routinely supplement fat soluble and water soluble vitamins at levels above suggested requirements, so the need for on-site supplementation is probably not necessary.

Regardless, always consult with your veterinarian before deciding to supplement vitamins in your horse's diet.

When we are blessed with an invitation into the equine world we experience a sense of peace and calmness of a simpler less complicated time. Stepping into an atmosphere of uncomplicated is a much welcomed and required counterbalance to the stress and weight of the demands and angst of this 'modern' world of instant everything.

It is our responsibility to ensure this harried world of immediate need of instant everything does not get passed the stall doors. The horse's digestive system is one of delicate balance and worthy of the time it takes to ensure optimal wellness.

Sheighlyn and Blondie head to head

Chapter IX

A dog may be man's best friend, but the horse wrote his history...unknown

Fruits and Veggies

I feed my horses a variety of fruits and vegetables. I just love showing up at the stalls with my pockets full of cut up pieces of fruit and veggies....I am soooo loved. I am so into bribery. No pushing and shoving allowed though. They all know no manners means no rewards.

Just like for my two-legged family usage, fruits and veggies for my horses are also rinsed in vinegar/water solution and then rinsed with clean water to remove pesticides and fungicides. Never offer produce starting to go bad. Horses are very sensitive to molds, bacteria and contaminants.

In the wild horses use the extra moisture in fruit and grass to supplement water intake. It's been advocated that giving watermelon (both the rind and the flesh) will cool down a horse and help prevent a heat stroke while passion fruit is said to have a calming effect on horses.

I've offered both to my babies....the passion fruit was a hit with few of them while seedless watermelon, providing the rind was attached, was a bigger hit but, by no means unanimous. Of course these remedies are absolutely dependant on whether or not watermelon and passion fruit sit on your horse's top 10 list of favourite foods.

It's suggested that fruits and veggies should be cut into strips not chunks (bigger danger of getting lodged in the throat) to avoid choking. It's also not recommended to feed horse's seeds or pips from fruit because of trace amounts of cyanide.

This news became a bit of a conundrum for me because Cider River Ranch was, back in the day, an old apple farm. There still remains apple and pear trees right in the middle of what has now become their grazing fields. Come harvest time I'm picking bags of apples/pears from trees and the ground. Do I get them all? To my chagrin and their pleasure, that would be nope....especially after a summer storm and they get there before I do.

In spite of my efforts, they still consume a fair number of apples and pears, seeds and all. In 14 years, here at Cider River Ranch there have been no issues with the consumption of this bounty as it lies in their fields of opportunity.

The harvest of the fruits are cut, quartered, de-seeded, frozen and enjoyed during those long cold winter months in the beet pulp supplement and homemade treats. Everyone is just happy, happy and I save a lot on the grocery bill. And that makes me happy, happy!

If in the wild and stumbled on a grove of fruit trees, horses would definitely hoover through the stash on the ground seeds and all.

Feeding fruits and veggies to a horse that has foundered is not recommended as this could be the result of an excess of carbohydrates. You should always consult your veterinarian first.

Just like in humans, fruits rich in antioxidants can help to destroy free radicals in horses. While succulents such as fruit and vegetables are useful for encouraging horses and ponies to eat their feed, it's important to ensure that your horse is receiving an overall balanced diet containing all nutrients require for good health. But, a slice of apple, pear or carrot is still a much healthier treat and learning motivator than a sugary mint.

Apples – *an apple a day keeps the vet away....*

Apples clean the teeth and strengthen the gums; reduce cholesterol levels; detoxify; contains antiviral properties; prevents constipation as it aids digestion for both horse and rider.

Ensure the apples are washed thoroughly with vinegar/water solution and then rinsed in cold water to remove all insecticides and pesticides before feeding.

Canadian researchers found the Red Delicious and Northern Spy contain more disease-fighting antioxidants in their skin and flesh. For you and your horse, it would appear red is the colour of choice.......just saying!

Be it for human or equine, studies suggest components of the apple are essential for normal growth, development and overall well-being.

Health benefits of apple for your horse

- Rich in Vitamin C and beta-carotene; powerful natural antioxidant.
- Rich in fibre; supports colon health
- Low glycemic levels
- Rich in antioxidants, including Vitamin E and various enzymes that protect from oxidative damage caused by free radicals.
- Low in calories.....excellent choice for those fatty patties and chunkie hunkies!!
- Contain no saturated fats or cholesterol.
- Contain B-complex vitamins, ie riboflavin, thiamin, pyridoxine (vit B-6)
- Contains low amounts of potassium, phosphorus and calcium

Bonus Health benefits of Apple particular to the human condition – all of the above plus:

- Regular eating aids healing of gout and rheumatism. Eating two apples a day reduces cholesterol levels up to 10%.

- An apple eaten prior to meals decreases indigestion; grated apple mixed with yogurt helpful with diarrhea
- Rich in Flavinoids; special nutrient found primarily in skin of apple (red apples in particular) helps prevent blood clots; regulates blood pressure and cholesterol levels; helps prevent growth of prostate cancer cells; so don't be too quick to peel that apple.
- Lowers need for insulin and thereby helps control diabetes

Asparagus - *Yes, you can share this great veggie with your horse!*

You will appreciate the nutrients so beneficial to you are just as beneficial to your horse. Because of its strange smell not all horses will take a liking to this veggie. It is recommended that only one to two pieces per day be offered to your horse as green vegetables tend to produce gas. Horses will regulate their own intake when asparagus grows wild in fields.

Asparagus can be green, white and purple in colour. Purple colored is higher in sugar but never-the-less healthy to eat. I like to pick out rounded thin but firm asparagus stalks as they tend to be tender and juicy. Fat or twisted stalks can be tough and woody to the disconcerting.

I wrap the asparagus ends in a damp paper towel, put in a Tupperware container and store in my refrigerator.

Health Benefit of Asparagus for your horse

- High content of Vitamin K and folic acid with fiber, folate, vitamins A, C, E, K and Chromium
- Packed with antioxidants that assist in destruction of cell-damaging free radicals.
- Cleanses and strengthen gastrointestinal tract and colon – natural detoxifies
- Anti-inflammatory and diuretic properties (treats arthritis, asthma (heaves))
- Helps relieve constipation – considered a laxative
- Helps in production of milk for lactating mothers (both human and equine)

Bonus Health Benefits of Asparagus Particular to the Human Condition – all of the above plus:

- Lowers LDH cholesterol significantly and also reduces high blood pressure
- Cleansing and detoxifying of kidneys prevent kidney stones and urinary tract infections
- Antioxidants also help slow down the aging process
- Helps to increase the success and recovery rate of chemotherapy
- Helps to relieve menstrual cramps, water retention and PMS
- Helps to strengthen capillaries thus preventing painful varicose veins
- Discourages wart growth
- Aphrodisiac properties that enhance intimacy

My horses graze in fields in which asparagus grows wild. They just help themselves. How lucky is that? In the wild, it has been determined, horses instinctively know what plants to eat for medicinal purposes. Domesticated they depend on us to know.

Asparagus becomes a seasonal delicacy for my crew as it would be over my grocery budget to buy this more expensive veggie for seven horses plus the family. Because it grows in my fields, I needed to know the impact this would have on my babies. Was so happy to learn it was all good?

Banana – *hooves down a favourite treat*

Athletes snack on bananas between matches/sets for an energy boost and added potassium. Equestrians feed their mounts a banana at competitions for the same reason.

Bananas are like candy to horses and they love to eat them skin on, so you don't even have to peel one. Cut in slices, skin and all!

I had no idea bananas do not grow on trees. Neither did I know the banana plant is classified as an arborescent (tree-like) perennial herb and the banana itself is actually considered a berry. The correct name for bunch of bananas is a hand of bananas; a single banana is a finger. Who knew! Okay, now we are so ready for those fifth graders.

Health Benefits of Banana for your horse

- Great source of phosphorous, calcium, iron, vitamin A, vitamin C, niacin, vitamin E and vitamin B6
- Low glycemic level
- More calories (energy) than an apple, but less sugar
- Contain lots of potassium, essential for cardiac health

Bonus Health Benefits Of Bananas particular to the Human Condition –all of the above plus:

- Contains high levels of tryptophan which is converted into serotonin and norepinephrine; prevents depression by encouraging feelings of well-being and relaxation
- Eat two bananas before a strenuous workout to pack an energy punch and sustain your blood sugar
- Strengthen your blood and relieve anemia with the added iron from bananas
- Bananas contain 16% of the daily recommended dietary fiber which helps you with digestion, prevents colon cancer and is good for your digestion in general
- Natural antacid, providing relief from acid reflux, heartburn and GERD
- Bananas are high in antioxidants, providing free radicals and protection from chronic disease
- Eating bananas helps prevent kidney cancer, protects the eyes against macular degeneration and builds strong bones by increasing calcium absorption

- Healthy source of carbohydrates (energy); curbs the appetite throughout the day
- Vitamin B6 reduces swelling, protects against type II diabetes, aids weight loss, strengthens the nervous system, and helps with the production of white blood cells and hemoglobin (red blood cells)

Found this interesting bit of information. At the 2000 Olympics bananas were fed to horses by a number of competing countries including the Australian dressage horse Crisp.

Carrots – *your honey bunny's all time favourite snack food!*

Carrot plant is cultivated across the world for its prized taproot. The whole plant is harvested when the root reaches about an inch in diameter, tender and juicy. Grown in Europe, Asia and North America carrots are a welcomed treat for your horse but not in huge amounts.

Recommend no more than four to five carrots a day for horses suffering with Cushings Disease, insulin resistance or EPSM (equine polysaccharide storage myopathy).

Wash carrots thoroughly and never feed if old or moldy. Slicing the carrots into slices eliminates any danger of large chunk lodging in the esophagus of the horse.

Carrots are low in fat and calories and high in fiber. They are high in essential nutrients, low in sodium and no cholesterol, making carrots a great snack with staying power.

If the horse is a fussy eater or has gone off his food for some reason, such as the stress of competition, adding carrots to his/her food adds tasty variety and encourages eating.

Introduce any new feed to a horse gradually over a period of time. The microbes within the digestive system must be allowed to adjust to the new feed.

So, if you have a 1,000-pound plus carrot-lovin' "funny honey bunny" in your barn, don't worry...they are as good for him as they are for you.

Health benefits of carrots for your horse

- Rich in anti-oxidants, vitamins and dietary fiber
- High in Vitamin C and K; healthy levels of minerals – copper, calcium, potassium, manganese and phosphorus
- Rich in many B-complex groups of vitamins such as folic acid, Vitamin B-6, thiamine

Bonus Health Benefits Particular of Carrots to the Human Condition – all of the above plus:

- Exceptionally rich source of carotenes and Vitamin A; promotes healthy eyes, intestinal and urinary tracts and mucous membranes
- Major carotene present is beta carotene; one of the most powerful natural anti-oxidant helps protect from harmful oxygen-free radical injury

Pumpkin - Pumpkin for your pumpkin!

Your horse will love the sweet taste and juicy texture. You will love what the nutrients can do for you and your horse.

Look for mature product that features fine woody note on tapping, heavy in hand and dry, stout stem. Avoid the one with wrinkled surface, cuts and bruises. Fully ripen pumpkin can be stored for many weeks at room temperature in cool, well-ventilated place. Cut sections keep well for few days when stored in refrigerator.

Wash thoroughly in a vinegar/water solution, then rinse in cold water to remove dust, soil and any residual insecticides/ fungicides before cutting and deseeding.

Chop the pumpkin into pieces manageable for your horse. Horses can eat pumpkin rind.

While most literature speaks against feeding fruit seeds to horses, vegetable seeds present as more digestible. Do not advise giving handfuls of seeds to your horse but a few pumpkin seeds that come along with the preparation of the pumpkin would be acceptable.

I have dried out pumpkin seeds for human consumption. I have also been known to grind some of these seeds in an old coffee grinder. Would use ground pumpkin seeds when making horse treats. From time to time would sprinkle on Blondie's feed when she would stick her nose in the air to the feed offered. Worked like a charm.

I have used pumpkin puree if pumpkin is out of season for making treats, as a disguise for giving medication and, from time to time, mixed in the soaked winter feed of beet pulp as a supporter of a healthy pooping machine. So don't be quick to squash the idea of squash for your horse.

Health benefits of Pumpkin for your horse

- Presence of Zinc; boosts the immune system and improves bone density.
- Presence of powerful antioxidants
- Rich in carotenoids; keeps immune system strong and healthy.
- Rich in fibre; helps maintain healthy bowel system
- Rich in potassium (essential electrolyte); helps maintain healthy heart

Bonus Health Benefits Particular of Pumpkin to the Human Condition –all of the above plus:

- Presences of anti-inflammatory agents that help prevent plaque/cholesterol build up on arterial walls and decrease risk of stroke.
- Rich in alpha-carotene; slows age-related poor eye sight; prevents cataract formation; reduces the risk of macular degeneration
- Lowers blood pressure

Dandelion Greens – *yummie in the tummie*

I openly admit I had no idea of the benefits of the dreaded dandelion. Had heard rumours of its usefulness but sadly didn't take the dandelion seriously. I was always on guard with a garden claw. Still am, but with a different focus to the dandelion hunt.

Dandelion greens can be found at health food stores, co-ops and farmers markets. It's recommend that you purchase unblemished, dark green leaves.

Dandelion in the spring can be found in grazing fields and in your own back yard. When foraging, harvest young greens before the flower heads appear (less bitter). Be sure to wash thoroughly especially if insecticides/pesticides have been used.

The leaves are highly perishable. Leaves should be stored in the refrigerator in a large plastic tub with a piece of paper towel to absorb excess moisture. Keeps 2 – 4 days.

Health Benefits of Dandelion Greens for your horse

- High in dietary fiber, Vitamins A, C, E, K, thiamin, riboflavin, Vitamin B6, calcium, iron, potassium, manganese, folate, magnesium, phosphorus and copper
- High in anti-oxidant vitamins
- Rich source of vitamin K required for bone mass building
- Fresh leaves low in calories
- Great source of nutrition during winter
- Limit amount in diet if interested in weight gain.
- Ideal for maintaining optimum health and weight loss

<u>Bonus Health Benefits of Dandelion Greens Particular to the Human Condition</u> – all of the above plus:

- Treatment of Alzheimer's disease by limiting neuronal damage in the brain
- Low in saturated fat and cholesterol

<u>Grapes</u> - *Yes, you and your horses can enjoy seedless grapes!*

While there is evidence to suggest that grapes are toxic to dogs, there is no problem in feeding grapes to horses. In fact, due to their small size grapes make an excellent treat to carry around with you when riding, brushing or spending time with your horse.

A great way to feed grapes to horses, especially in the summer, is to freeze them so they are more crunchy and unusual for your horse.

Only use seedless grapes. Wash thoroughly in vinegar/water solution and then rinse in cold water to remove bacteria and/or pesticides.

Because of high sugar content should be integrated into a balanced diet as occasional treats once or twice a week at most. But given the high cost of grapes this becomes a rare and welcomed treat for my crew. The rarity occurs when the sales occur. Freezing them is just a bonus for all of us. Not to mention my pocket book!

Health Benefits of Grapes for your horse

- Rich source of Vitamin C; antioxidant that helps fight free radicals that can harm
- Excellent source of Vitamin B1 helps provide energy and keeps nervous system healthy and functioning correctly
- High concentration of Manganese.
- Contributes to strong, healthy bones.
- Helps connective tissue to develop and form.
- Helps with absorption of Calcium.
- Promotes weight loss

Bonus Health Benefits of Grapes Particular to the Human Condition – all of the above plus:

- Flavonnoids contained in grapes helps reduce blood clots that can cause strokes, heart attacks and poor circulation.
- Rich calcium content help delay bone loss
- Potassium helps avoid high blood pressure and stroke

Pears - *share the pear between the pair of you!*

Pears can become the favorite treat of your horse. They are so sweet and juicy.

Horses tend to prefer the sweet juice of the very ripe, squidgy pears but ensure your pears aren't old, moldy or rotten!

Thoroughly wash the pear in vinegar/water solution rinse well in cold water to remove bacteria and pesticides. Remove the seeds and slice into thin long slices.

The Pear is revered as the most hypoallergenic fruit. Medicine dissolved in pear juice can be given to your horse in a syringe (or mixed in feed). Pear juice also reduces a fever and helps the medicine go down for the rider as well.

I will take the pears that grow here at Cider River Ranch remove the seeds, cut and quarter and freeze them for use in the winter feed. I also will put some through my juicer and freeze the juice for later use as well.

The pear offers so many benefits all good to know whether it's for horse or rider.

Health benefits of Pears for your horse

- Rich in **Vitamin C**; antioxidant properties protecting cells from free radicals.
- High in fibre; good for horses digestive system
- Presence of antioxidants; strengthens the immune system and lowers risk of age-related vision loss
- Presence of Boron; helps retain calcium, lowers risk of osteoporosis and increase bone density.
- Presence of Foliate; prevents neural tube defects of fetus.
- Low calorie fruit; good for weight loss
- Rich **fibre** content; prevents constipation, promotes regularity and good colon health

- Presence of fructrose/glucose (found in pear juice); source of healthy energy; relieves pain in inflammatory conditions

Bonus Health Benefits of Pears Particular to the Human Condition – all of the above plus:

- Rich **pectin** content; helps lower cholesterol, blood pressure and risk of stroke

SAFE fruits and vegetables: (Providing horse has no health problems)

Apricots, beets, beetroot, blackberries, blueberries, celery, cherries (pits removed), coconut, parsnip, corncob without the corn (cut in slices), dates, figs (pitted), green beans, lettuce, mangoes, melon rinds including watermelon, honeydew and cantaloupe flesh, passion fruit, peaches (pitted), peas, peppermints, raspberry, rutabaga, raisins, squash, pumpkin, strawberries, sweet potatoes, sprouts (alfalfa, wheat, barley), sugar cubes.

Tidbit to consider. Next trip to the supermarket when browsing the produce aisle, keep your horse in mind. He may enjoy (and benefit) from more than you think.

Unsafe fruits and vegetables: (Will create health problems for your horse)

Avocado, broccoli or cauliflower, cabbage (may cause gas – may cause colic), citrus based fruits, chocolate, garlic, kale, onions, potatoes, persimmons, rhubarb, tomatoes, any members of the nightshade family (which includes peppers, sweet and hot peppers), eggplant, paprika, and cayenne peppers.

Bread, cooked rice – insulin resistance problems; prone to equine Cushing's disease

Absolutely no meat products or by products as horses are herbivores and their digestive system is not designed to metabolize meat.

Best rule of thumb for anything....when in doubt don't...in this case just doesn't feed it to your horse. Always do your own research and consult with your veterinarian.

Chapter X

If you want a stable friendship, get a horse. ...Unknown

Mother Nature's Most Perfect Foods

I'm going to dedicate a small section of Creature Comforts for Horses to Mother Nature's two most perfect foods, coconut and honey.

In recent years with the introduction of oil to the horse's diet, the benefits of coconut oil and coconut meal in the horse's diet has proven to be a huge bonus to the overall health and performance of the horse. I'm not going to go into great deal on either food source other than to speak of the benefits they offer.

Finding feeds containing coconut meal or coconut oil has proven difficult in my neck of the woods. My search took me to the website of Stance Equine. Dr. Tim Kempton is a well known respected Australian horseman. He is also a highly regarded scientist.

Dr. Kempton has been involved, for over 20 years, in the research and production of coconut as horse feed. If you research Dr. Kempton and his company Stance Equine you can read for yourself the benefits of coconut in the equine diet. From there it's easy to discover other research into this marvelous plant also validating its worth to the equine world.

Coconut Meal and Oil

Both coconut meal and coconut oil provide important nutritional elements for horses. Both the coconut meal and oil are high in protein with the meal having higher fiber content. But, the main reason for adding it to an equine diet is for the fat content.

Coconut meal has relatively high protein content but because it is low in lysine it is not the same quality as found in more common protein sources such as soybean meal.

Coconut meal's digestible energy content is in the same range as beet pulp or soy hulls higher in fiber and lower in NSC. Coconut meal contains less than 2% starch (non-structural carbohydrates) and does not cause the same starch related issues such as tying up and laminitis.

Saturated oils are derived from animal fats or coconut oil. Animal fats are unacceptable in horse feeds. Coconut oil is a palatable source of saturated fatty acids for our horses.

Coconut oil is high in protein, fiber and fat content and makes this an ideal food component for your horse's diet. Coconut oil is no different than any other high fat product fed to horses. It too is energy dense and yields about 2 times more energy than starch or protein. It actually gives your

84

horse an easy digestible energy source without the "hotness" associated with high grain diets.

Early when discussing saturated fats, triglycerides where identifed as the most common lipid found in the horse's body. Coconut was also identified as a saturated fat with medium chain triglycerides (MCT).

MCT is absorbed more rapidly and is metabolized quicker than the long chain triglycerides found in vegetable oil, soy oil and corn oil. Rather than being stored for fat, the body converts the MCT into fuel for muscles.

Studies have shown that saturated fatty acids of coconut oil have had the following effects on our horses. They increase muscle glycogen content, increase sparing of muscle glycogen during light work and increase the usage of muscle glycogen during heavy work. Whereas unsaturated oils such as rice bran, corn, soybean and flax do not give these effects.

All of this makes coconut oil remarkably beneficial to horses that need "long burn energy" such as performance horses. Because coconut oil provides the medium chain triglycerides (MCT) and not the long chain triglycerides of other plant oil sources, coconut oil is also a terrific fat source for horses with metabolic imbalances such as insulin resistance and Cushings disease.

Another bonus of coconut oil is that is very stable and resistant to rancidity. Because of its saturated structure, coconut oil can be stored for long periods of time without risk of rancidity.

Rancid oils reduce the palatability of a feed, interfere with the utilization of fat soluble vitamins and may cause damage to muscle and organ tissue if consumed.

Now, if that isn't enough the bonus of coconut oil is the MCT of coconut oil contains the fatty acid lauric. Mother's milk is the only other source of this amazing fatty acid. The boost to the immune system is just awesome.

Finally, most horses seem to love the taste of coconut so it's another great disguise for the less palatable supplements and medications. Not to mention it adds a shine to the coat.

Honey

Although honey is neither a fruit nor veggie it can be a potentially helpful remedy of certain ailments. As you read you will see the topic of honey is probably a little more relevant to the human condition as opposed to that of the equine.

But, as stated previously, I believe the health and well being of the owner/rider impacts the world of the horse every bit as much as the health and well being of the horse impacts that of the own/rider. There becomes a melding of these two worlds and all emotions are shared.

Honey is considered the only food to contain all the substances necessary for sustaining life and therefore often described as Mother Nature's most perfect food. Honey was the most used medicine in ancient Egypt.

The great Napoleon used the bee as a symbol of his empire. During World War I, honey was mixed with cod liver oil and used to treat the wounds of soldiers.

Without the honey bee and its mission to pollinate plant life for future generations, there would be no life.

Scientific research at University of California reported in March 2004 daily consumption of honey improves the immune system by raising antioxidant levels in blood thereby reducing risk of free radical damage.

Dr Ihor Basko, DVM. Dr. Basko is considered the leading authority in the USA on holistic animal health. Dr. Basko graduated from Michigan State University veterinarian med program. Within his practice and teachings, Dr. Basko amalgamates traditional care and alternative homeopathic therapies.

Dr. Basko stated he adopted holistic medicine into his practice because it focused on the true nature of healing – prevention of chronic disease. An ounce of prevention is still worth more than a pound of cure.

Health Benefits of Honey for horses (Dr. I. Basko renown homeopathic veterinarian)

- Only use honey when necessary since horses in the wild would have little to no access to honey; consider one to two tablespoons every 2 – 3 days a safe amount.

- Can be used to medically treat constipation, malnutrition, weakness and some allergies
- In dry climates where grass very dry, honey can be used to improve digestion and evacuation of manure and possibly prevent colic.
- Honey can boost the immune system.
- Recommends horses insulin resistance, have foundered or susceptible to founder should not be fed honey, fruits, veggies or other horse treats without veterinarian consultation.

Bonus Health Benefits of Honey Particular to the Human Condition

- The mixture of equal quantities of honey and ginger juice is a good expectorant. It helps treat colds, cough, sore throat and a runny nose.
- Honey can soothe and encourage the healing of sores in the mouth or vagina.
- A bowl of oats or porridge with a spoonful of honey can calm the nerves. It is ideal for fighting pre-exam stress.
- Honey is a great moisturizer and can be used on the skin as a natural revitalizing mask.
- Eating a little local honey will make you "immune" to pollen in the area.
- To improve eyesight, mix honey with carrot juice. Take one hour before meals in the morning.
- To purify the blood, mix one glass of warm water with one to two teaspoons of honey and one teaspoon of lemon juice. It will also reduce fat and

cleanse your bowels. Take this preparation daily before going to the toilet.

- Natural honey causes a lower rise in blood sugar than refined sugars in people with type-II diabetes.
- A little unprocessed honey can be added in the drinks of type-II diabetics when they crave sweetness.
- Daily piece of toast with unpasteurized honey sprinkled with cinnamon helps reduce blood pressure.
- Honey has sedative properties.
- It is anti-fungal and nourishing.
- It soothes tissues and helps retain calcium in the body.
- Honey is an antibacterial, great for both internal and external problems.
- It is considered to be the Swiss army knife in the world of alternative medicine.

Chapter XI

There is no bond stronger than that between horse and rider...unknown

RECIPES

Oats and hay are fine for the feed bucket but healthy treats can add variety and vitamins to your equine friend's diet as well.

Aside from demonstrated affection and gratitude towards you, your horse will benefit from the same antioxidants, anti-inflammatory and energy-boosting nutrition and vitamins you enjoy.

So stave off boredom on the bridle trail, or reward for a job well done, or just because the giving of a judicious, nutritious selection of fruits and vegetables for a mount with a discerning palate is always a welcoming gesture of love.

Have fun with the recipes. Add the fruits and vegetables compatible to horse consumption and your horse's preference. Feel free to play with the recipes. Creating your own custom cookie is more than half the fun. More so if you share the experience with a junior rider!

Incorporating those delicious fruits and veggies into scrumptious treats becomes priceless for the steed with astute taste and a desire to become an equine treat connoisseur, and you his favourite chef. From my kitchen here at Cider River Ranch to your kitchen.....**Bon appétit!**

Blondie inhaling the aroma of fresh baked super sized horse treat!

1. Blondie's Blossom's

Ingredients: **Preparation: Time 15 minutes**

- 1 ½ cups oatmeal (quick oats)   Preheat oven to
- 1 cup flour   350F
- 2 finely chopped Turkish figs
- 1 mashed banana
- 2 tbsp molasses
- 1 cup unsweetened apple sauce
- Water (add enough to make dough doughy
- Mix all these ingredients together to make doughy dough

Make small dough balls; flatten balls on parchment paper covered cookie sheet, then

- 1 finely chopped apple   Mix finely chopped apple; cinnamon;
- 1 tbsp cinnamon   brown sugar together with enough hot
- 2 tbsp brown sugar   water to melt mixture, then

Drizzle brown sugar/cinnamon and chopped apple mixture over each cookie!

Bake for 15 – 20 minutes (until golden brown). Slight spongy texture to cookie but very yummy!!!!

NOTES

2.   Apache's Apple Awesome

Ingredients: **Preparation: Time 15 minutes**

- 2 cups unsweetened applesauce*   Preheat oven to 350F
- 1 cup rolled oats
- 1 cup flour   Oil 9x9 square cake
- 1 shredded carrot   pan (I use coconut oil)
- 2 tbsp molasses   Mix all ingredients
                                     together
- 5 finely chopped pitted dates   Spread batter evenly in
                                     cake pan

Bake for 20 – 30 minutes. The batter will start to shrink away from the sides of pan. Cake will be firm to touch. Allow to cool and cut into squares.

*buy apples when in season (cheaper); make applesauce and freeze for baking.

Definitely a triple "A" treat that will win you all the Adoration, Accolades and Admiration you desire....

NOTES

Catman's Eat More's

Ingredients:	Preparation: 30 - 45 min
• 1 cup uncooked oats	Preheat oven at 350F
• 1 cup grated carrots	
• 1 cup grated apples	Mix ingredients in bowl except water
• 1 cup flour	Doughy mixture should be little sticky
• ½ cup sweet feed (12%)	
• 1 tsp sea salt	
• ½ cup pumpkin puree	Use hand or mellon scoop to make balls
• 2 tbsp coconut oil (melt)	
• 1 mashed banana	
• 1 – 2 tbsp unpasteurized honey (or molasses)	
• ½ cup water enough to make dough a little sticky	Place on greased or parchment paper covered cookie sheet

Bake for 15 minutes or light brown.

Can't just have one....'more please' will be the look!

NOTES

Chance's Chosen Cookie

Ingredients: **Preparation: 15 minutes**

- 1 cup flour
- ½ cup sweet feed (12%)   Preheat oven for 350 degrees F
- 2 mashed bananas
- 1/4 cup coconut oil (melt)   Mix all ingredients together
- 2 tbsp unpasteurized honey   Stir until well blended; thicken with more flour;
- 1 apple; 1 pear grated   thin with banana and/or oil
- Crushed mints   Mixture should be sticky not runny

Drop bite size batter onto parchment paper covered cookie sheet

Bake: 10 – 20 min. Should be crunchy when done. Cool and store in fridge.

Excellent reward for a good workout!!

NOTES

Cake Boss Birthday Cake....horsey style

Ingredients: **Preparation: Time 25 minutes**

- 4 cups quick oats
- 1 mashed ripe banana
- ½ cup shredded carrots
- ½ cup shredded apples
- 2 tbsp unpasteurized honey
- 4-6 peppermints (crushed)
- ¼ cup molasses
- Water

Preheat oven at 350F

Mix oatmeal, ripe banana, carrots, apples

Mix in honey and molasses

Add water 1 tbsp at a time until semi-mushy not sloppy

Press firmly into a 9x9 cake pan. Sprinkle top with crushed peppermint

Bake for 30 minutes. Cool. Cut up and divide with all those at the birthday party.

Bring on the 'wow factor'. Print out age on top of cake with peppermints. Bang it up a notch and become the cake boss. Use carrot sticks as candles, apple pieces as decoration.

NOTES

Foxy Lady's Diva Dining

Ingredients: **Preparation: Time 20 minutes**

- 1 cup oatmeal
- 1 cup shredded carrots or apples
- 1 cup flour
- 1 tsp sea salt
- 1 – 2 tbsp pasteurized honey
- ¼ cup water
- ¼ cup organic molasses

Preheat oven 350F

Mix all ingredients in large bowl

Make bite-sized balls

Place on greased/ parchment covered cookie sheet

Bake for 15 - 20 minutes or until golden brown.

Divine. Absolutely divine

NOTES

"It's My Party"......Birthday Cake for Horses

Ingredients: Preparation: Time 20 minutes

- 4 cups rolled oats

- ¼ cup honey
- 1 tbsp molasses
- Puree ½ cup blueberries and
  ½ cup strawberries

- 2 carrots cut into carrot sticks
- 1 apple cut into slices

Mix honey, pureed berries and rolled oats

Place mixture on plate and shape form of cake

Let stand overnight in refrigerator then decorate!!

Use carrots as candles; apple, strawberry and blueberry as decoration

No crying at this party.... lip smacking enjoyment of the favourite present received.

NOTES

Jenny's "Who'da Thunk It" Horse Salad

Ingredients: **Preparation: Time 20 minutes**

- 6 apples   Slice fruit and veggies
                              into bite size slices

- 8 carrots
- 1 pear
- 2 cups chopped dandelion or   Chop dandelion
  Lettuce leaves   leaves (lettuce) bite size
                                  pieces
- ½ cup unsweetened coconut   Combine fruit, veggies,
                                dandelion leaves
- Molasses   and coconut together
- 4 Crush peppermints   Fold in enough molasses
                                to make coconut and
                                dandelion leaves stick
                                to fruit and veggies

Sprinkle crushed peppermints over mixture and fold in lightly. Chill overnight and serve

Ideal for the weight watchers in the crowd!

NOTES

Little Jasmine's 'Jump for Joy' Cookies

Ingredients: **Preparation: Time 20 minutes**

- 1 cup uncooked oats

    Preheat oven to 350F

- 1 cup flour Mix all ingredients together
- 1 cup shredded carrots
- Puree 1 pear with ¼ cup water

    Make "meatball" size balls place on greased

- 1 tsp sea salt

    (or parchment paper covered) cookie sheet

- 2 tbsp unpasteurized honey or molasses
- 2 tsp olive oil or coconut oil (melt)

Bake for 15 – 18 minutes until golden brown. Cool. Serve. The smaller the "meatball" the crispier the cookie otherwise expect a more soft chewie cookie with medium to large sized "meatball"!

Be the favourite human at the stalls!!!!

NOTES

Miss Callisto's Craving junior rider easy – microwave required

Ingredients: **Preparation: Time 15 min**

Ingredients	Preparation
• 2 cups flour	Mix all ingredients in a bowl
• 5 cups oatmeal	Make small balls
• ½ cup olive oil or coconut oil (melt)	Place on microwaveable plate
• 1 tbsp liquid honey	Flatten balls
• 1 cup of shredded carrots	Place in microwave

Bake on high for 6 minutes per batch.

Be a hero. Satisfy the cravings

NOTES

Ms Christine's Coin Cookies*

Ingredients:	Preparation: Time 2 hrs
• 1 cup sweet feed (12%)	Bake at 300F
• 1 cup bran	
• 1 cup flour	Mix molasses, honey, carrots and
• 4 large carrots, shredded	applesauce in bowl
• ½ cup molasses	Mix dry ingredients in another bowl
• 2 tbsp unpasteurized honey	Slowly combine molasses with dry
• 1 cup applesauce	Add enough molasses mixture to form a
• 2 tbsp brown sugar	thick dough (add more flour if necessary)

Line a cookie sheet with aluminum foil. (I prefer parchment paper)

Using a tablespoon, drop spoonfuls of batter onto cookie sheet. Flatten to form 'silver dollar' shaped cookies.

Bake for approx 50 to 60 minutes then flip and bake for additional 30 to 40 minutes. Depending on your oven, can reduce oven temperature to 250 for last 40 minutes. Cookies should be dried out but not burnt!!!

Labour of love for your four legged confidante will always be appreciate. Priceless!!!!!

NOTES

'Now Your Talkin' Bars

Ingredients:	Preparation: Time 15 minutes
• 2 cups oatmeal	Preheat oven at 350F
• ¾ cup grain (sweetfeed 12%)	
• 2 cups bran	Mix oats, grain and bran together
• 1 cup molasses	Drizzle in molasses while mixing with your hands to get consistency little thinner than Play-doh Place dollups onto cookie sheet

Bake for 10 minutes. Watch closely. Have tendency to burn. Never get completely hard.

Generates more whinnying than you could imagine

NOTES

Nugget's Notion of "Nice' Younger rider easy bake

Ingredients: Preparation: Time 20 min

- 1 cup rolled oats
- ¼ cup water

Mix rolled oats and water

Add honey and **smooth** peanut butter*

- ¼ cup of 12% sweet feed
- 1 carrot (cut in 1"-2" lengths)

Add favourite grain. Stir well

- 1 tsp of honey
- 1 tsp **smooth** peanut butter*

Roll carrot pieces in mixture to form ball (not too small)

Put carrot sticks in covered container in the refrigerator to harden. Then serve.

Voices become softer and movement more fluent when surrounded with nice....ask any horse!!!!

*check with your vet before giving peanut butter...research indicates smooth peanut butter okay but not chunky nor actual peanuts...may have difficulty passing through the digestive system!!!

NOTES

'One for the Bucket'
easy for young and mature riders

Ingredients: **Preparation: Time 20 minutes**

- 1 pkg Quaker oatmeal or 1 cup quick oatmeal   Can mix in feed bucket
- 1 cup sweet feed   Mix oatmeal and water
- ½ cup applesauce (unsweetened)   Add sweet feed and applesauce. Stir together
- 2 tbsp honey or molasses   Add cheerios, honey (or molasses)
- 1 cup Cheerios   Mix again
- ½ cup water (more or less)   Serves one horse

You can bet your soul connection will have this on his/ her bucket list

NOTES

Old Charlie's Favourite Cake

Ingredients: **Preparation: Time 15 minutes**

- 1 carrot   Preheat oven to 300F
- 1 apple
- ¼ cup of molasses   Grate the carrot and
  apple
- 2 1/2 cups oats   Mix together all
  ingredients
- ¼ cup coconut oil (melt) Place mixture in baking
  tray

Bake for 40 minutes or until golden brown. Cool for 4 hrs in refrigerator. Cut in desired pieces and serve.

Chuck full of Charlie's favourite things.....no anger management for this Charlie....makes the heart sing with palatable pleasure! Hmm hmm good!

NOTES

Old school Oats Molasses Cookies

Back in the day when there was just hay
Open fire, setting sun, day is over, job well done
Filled with desire to reward his steed
The cowboy thinks of what he would need
From the chuck wagon to a cast iron pan
Hmmm how those treats did tan
True to its roots and to this very day
The oat molasses cookie is here to stay

Ingredients: **Preparation: Time 15 minutes**

- 2 cups oatmeal
- ½ cup grated carrots
- ½ cup molasses

- 2 tbsp pasteurized honey
- Water

Preheat oven at 350F
Mix all ingredients together
Add enough water to make soft dough
Stir well
Roll out dough; cut shapes with cookie cutter
Place cookie shapes on parchment covered cookie sheet

Bake for 8 min. until golden brown (tan). Cool. Serve. Store in air-tight container

NOTES

Pj's Pleasure

Ingredients: **Preparation: time 20 minutes**

- 1 cup apples or carrots (or use ½ cup each)

  Preheat oven to 350F

- 1 cup oats

  Grate carrots; dice apples measure set aside

- 1 cup flour

  Mix together well oats, flour, salt and sugars

- 1 tsp salt

  Add carrots/apples

- 1 tbsp white sugar

  Mix in molasses and coconut oil

- 1 tbsp brown sugar

  Add ¼ water (as much need to make

- 2 tbsp coconut oil (melt)

  ingredients into a sticky dough not runny)

- ¼ cup molasses
- ¼ cup water

  Place tbsp dollops of batter on ungreased cookie sheet

Bake for 10 – 15 minutes. They won't change size; they will get firm. Crushed peppermint garnish on each cookie optional.

This little treat has proved to be an amazing motivator for the unmotivated!! Everyone is just happy, happy, happy!

NOTES

Rennie's Rhapsody

Ingredients: Preparation: Time 25 minutes

- 1 cup flour   Preheat oven to 325F
- 1 cup oats
- 1 cup water   Mix all ingredients together
- ½ cup finely   Form 1" (approx) balls
  chopped carrots
- ½ cup finely
  chopped apples
- 1/3 cup molasses   Place on parchment paper
                                     covered cookie sheet and
                                     flatten

- 1 tsp unpasteurized honey
- 1 tsp salt
- 2 tbsp coconut (melt) or olive oil
- 4 peppermint candies (crushed)

Bake for 20 minutes. Cool. Serve. Store in air tight container in refrigerator.

Oh joy! Oh bliss! This is one treat you do not want your horse to miss.

NOTES

Roxie's Regulation Reward – junior rider easy

Ingredients: **Preparation: Time 10 minutes**

- 4 cups bran

   Mix ingredients together **until** batter doughy

- 2 cups applesauce
- Puree 1 pear in blender

   Roll out with rolling pin
   Cut shapes with cookie cutter
   Let dough dry and serve

It is all good when emotional and physical needs are met at the same loving moment.

NOTES

Starv'n Marvin's Marvelous Munchies

Ingredients: Preparation: Time 15 minutes

- 1 cup dry oats   Preheat oven to 350F
- 1 cup shredded carrots
  and/or apples
- 1 cup finely chopped pear   Mix dry ingredients together,
                                   then
- 1 cup flour   Add remaining ingredients.
  Mix well
- 1 tsp salt
- 1 tbsp pastured honey   Drop tablespoon of mixture
                                   on greased
- 1/2 cup molasses   or parchment paper covered
                                   cookie sheet
- Little less than a
  1/4 cup water

Bake for 10 – 15 minutes (until golden brown). Store in air-tight container in fridge.

From picky finickity to bottomless pit this recipe is a crowd pleaser!

NOTES

Trail Treats

Ideal for the junior riders to make!!!

Ingredients: **Preparation: Time 20 – 25 min**

- 5 carrots cut in strips   Soak carrots for 15 minutes in large bowl
- ¼ cup molasses   Drain water and add molasses
- 2 cups oats or quick oats   Stir until carrots completely covered
- ½ cup 12% sweet feed   Mix in grains.
- Cold water

Roll each covered piece of carrot in oats. Wrap the carrot sticks in foil and freeze.

Great treat for the trail ride. The strips thaw while you ride.

Bonus Treats - wash seedless grapes (you chose the number); pat dry; put into freezer bag and then into your freezer. Great crunchy treat on a hot day.

NOTES

Chapter XII

A rider will have no joy if his horse does
not enjoy his work...H.H. Isenbart

Uncommon, common ailments

Again this is offered only as a gathering of information to broaden your knowledge base so when speaking of your horse to your veterinarian or farrier your questions are knowledge driven and not just fear driven.

Colic

In a baby or in a horse, colic is a belly ache. In our horses it is a really big bad belly ache. Colic is not a disease. Colic is the system of an acute digestive system issue.

The simplest form of colic is called 'spasmodic colic' of gas. Simply put, a portion of the bowel stops functioning correctly, gas builds up and the horse will feel "gas" pain.

Of course there are other reasons like parasites, bad feed/hay, lack of fresh water, bowel displacement, irritation by foreign debris in the gut, severe stress, staying too long in a confined space and the list can go on.

Suffice to say, lots of reasons for colic to present but the more serious causes of colic are impaction and/or infection irritating the bowel. Any time the symptoms of colic present in your horse the veterinarian must be called first as colic identifies a serious issue with the digestive system.

We know now this is a "one way only" system of, in the front door and out the back door and no ability to back up. If treatment is delayed, the more risk of death for your horse. I'm going to list the possible signs and symptoms of colic that may present in your horse.

- Behavioural/temperament changes
- May kick or bite at belly
- Abnormal postures
- Acts restless, pacing, pawing ground repeated lying and standing
- Stools may change as to amount, consistency, colour
- Coloration of gums and mouth may alter
- May grunt and groan
- Hyper increase of loud rumblings of belly; or no sound at all
- May put nose to water but not drink

The following are acts and actions we can take to help our horse while awaiting the arrival of the veterinarian. First and foremost, as always, safety for you and your horse is paramount. Stay calm and do not excite your horse. Stay alert and focused on your horses body language.

If possible, keep your horse on its feet and moving. Your calm, steady leadership is the best comfort for your horse.

Encourage your horse to drink by offering a bucket with 4-5 litres of warm water mixed with 2 -3 cups of bran and 1 cup of sweet feed. Make sure it is a very 'soupy' mixture so your horse can just slurp up the good stuff. It's the warm water with the bran that will simulate the peristalsis (movement) of the bowel...the sweet feed just helps the medicine go down and gives a boost to the energy level.

When calling your veterinarian answer and ask questions calmly and clearly in order to formulate a knowledge based plan to determine if this is a worst case scenario and not one that typically can resolves spontaneously and/or when assisted by the methods described above.

Never trailer a horse with suspected colic. Your vet will always come to you when signs and symptoms of colic present.

Diarrhea (Scours)

Scours is the term used to describe diarrhea in a horse. Although any horse can develop scours it is generally more common in foals and younger horses. It is an indicator something is wrong with the digestive system.

If your horse appears to be in pain, has pale gums, bites or kicks at his stomach or otherwise doesn't appear well, contact your veterinarian, can be the symptom of colic indicating there may be a serious issue with the digestive system requiring a consultation with your veterinarian sooner than later.

Scours can also be caused by changes in the diet such as sudden access to spring grass or diet changed to foods richer in some nutrients. Stop feeding the richer foods and feed quality hay. When the diarrhea clears up you can reintroduce the changes in the diet slowly and over time.

Every mammal learns to deal with and manage the stress of daily living. But it's that extra stress created when the stress of our daily living is exaggerated and we are powerless to stop the exaggeration. No more so than for our horses.

Decease in regular exercise and turnout because of injury or bad weather can lead to scours. Invest time hand-walking your horse several times a day to determine if this is the root evil.

Sometimes parasites are the root evil so try to deworm your horse on a regular basis. I know I'm preaching to the choir but this is said more for the benefit of the new beginner owner than the experienced seasoned owner.

Also consider resistance to worming medicine or improper technique could mean your horse didn't receive the correct dosage and may not be worm-free. Your veterinarian may want you to collect stool samples to determine if parasites are present.

A decrease in the required intestinal probiotics can lead to scours. This can occur due to stress, antibiotic treatment or infection. Probiotics provide needed intestinal bacteria that help with digestion. If your horse has experienced any of the above stated issues, consult your veterinarian and discuss adding probiotics to your horse's diet.

Make sure your horse has access to clean fresh water. Your horse will lose a lot of body fluid while enduring scours. Once the reason for scours is removed the diarrhea will clear up.

Heaves

Heaves is known as Recurrent Airway Obstruction (RAO) that can range from being a mild concern to a deadly problem. Sometimes is the result of eating dusty hay or stalled in a dusty stable. Sometimes is part of the aging processes.

The occasional runny nose and that sparotic nagging little cough, usually present at the beginning of your ride could mean your horse is the very early stages of recurrent airway obstruction (RAO). A condition commonly referred to as 'heaves'.

Heaves can never be cured and severe cases are difficult to manage but catching it early can help you manage it more effectively and possibly minimize damage to your horse's lungs.

Heaves is like asthma as it is an allergic-based disease interfering with your horse's ability to breathe properly. When your horse is exposed to allergy-producing particles in the air, such as dust and pollens, cells in his lungs react by releasing chemicals that cause air passage linings to swell, thicken, and produce mucous.

As your horse breathes, air gets trapped in the thick passages. Now your horse has to exert an effort to expel the 'trapped' air. Heaves is most common among mature and older horses. The excess mucous produced will often present as a "runny" discharge from the nose.

Symptoms of mild heaves to watch for are a flaring of the nostrils and a spontaneous cough. Coughing while eating or while barn is swept out. If you observe your horse displaying a decrease in his stamina and tolerance with a related cough when exercising suspect recurrent airway obstruction (RAO), heaves.

Symptoms of severe heaves include all of the above but you can now add respiratory distress, distinct heave lines over the chest wall together with audible wheezing and grunting to expel air.

Management of heaves is the only option. If possible keep your horse in grass pasture and not on dirt/dust. If stabled, keep in a well-ventilated and dust free stable. It would be better to keep your horse in a stall only if absolutely necessary. Always remove your horse from the stable before cleaning.

Consider your horse's diet is mostly hay and hay can be very dry and dusty. If possible soak hay before feeding or consider soaked hay cubes or pellets. Beet pulp and whole grains are dusty and should be served presoaked to any horse with heaves.

Heaves has become a topic of great concern for me and our 28 year old mare Blondie. Blondie is my heroine. As a young girl my daughter was bucked off a pony. With her foot caught in a stirrup she was dragged across a field. The back injuries haunt her to this day. Rescued by a fellow rider, she vowed never to ride again.

But then along came Blondie. A bomb proof, well trained all white appaloosa mare 16 hands high. Big girl so I wasn't sure how my daughter would react. It was a true union from the first moment they met. Blondie was gentle, patient and very tolerant of this fearfully hesitant young girl. Blondie allowed my daughter to overcome her fears and ride again. Blondie is so special.

When Blondie's episodes of heaves suddenly went from mild to severe last spring I went on a mission to develop a treatment plan that would reduce if not eliminate any further severe attacks. It was such a frightening, heartbreaking experience for both Blondie and us when she struggled and labored to breath.

I am not advocating anyone follow this plan. Do your own research. Speak with your vet and other equine health specialists. Make your own informed plan to counter heaves in your horse.

Growing thyme in my window sill garden made it easy for me to pop a sprig of it into my blender with fruit of choice (apple/pear rich in Vitamin C), 1 ½ tsp of ginger*, and ¼ cup of coconut oil and then enough water to make a smoothie consistency. I would then mix this with her daily feed of presoaked beet pulp and senior feed. I would divide her daily ration in half; add half of this smoothie to her 7 am feeding and the other half at 7 pm.

During the first week I had no hesitation to rub Vicks Vapour rub on and around her big beautiful nostrils.

Also I mix together 1 tbsp of Tumeric (anti-inflammatory spice); 1 tbsp of molasses and top with warm water in a litre spray bottle and soaked her hay.

This formula worked for Blondie. Within a day the acute respiratory symptoms abated and a month later, while still on this schedule, our Blondie started to regain weight. She no longer exhibited chest wall in drawing, nasal flaring and no more nasal drip. She still coughed occasionally but she was back to her to her normal demeanor of the queen.

*Ginger works on the respiratory system to cleanse and heal. The ginger has to be partially sliced and boiled and to ensure potency, should be crushed a bit before boiling.

All treatments should be discussed with your veterinarian before you implement them into your horse's diet.

Rain Rot

Rain rot or rain scald is also known as dermatophilosis is caused by a bacterial infection and it often is mistaken for fungal disease. According to The Merck Veterinary Manual, bacterium found to cause this infection lives dormant within the skin until the skin is compromised in some way. This can happen when there's prolonged wetness, high humidity, high temperature or attacks by biting insects, particularly flies and ticks.

Because bacteria live in the outer layer of skin, when the skin is compromised this can cause inflamed, red infected scabs to form ranging in size from pinpoint to large crusty scabs. Fluid filled scabbing lesions develop causing surrounding skin to become matted. Coat develops rough appearance and you will be able to feel small lumps on horse's skin when running your hand over the coat.

As the lesions get larger and join together, they will progress to a crust or scab formation. It starts to feel like a coat of armour. When these scabs are removed yellow/green pus is exposed between the necrotic and living skin layers. When rubbed, the "lumps" will come off in the form of scabs exposing hairless inflamed areas of skin.

Most cases of rain rot can heal on its own. However it is recommended even minor cases are treated as the lesions can spread and become worse. Unlike a lot of skin conditions, rain rot is not itchy but it can be very painful for your horse when touched so be careful when bathing or removing the scabs.

Bathing your horse with antimicrobial shampoo and currying will take care of the problem. More severe cases in which the infection has affected deeper skin layers will require your veterinarian for antibiotics like penicillin or streptomycin.

Wash hands thoroughly in order to avoid accidental contamination to surroundings areas. Clear affected area by clipping away hair. Gently clean area with clean fresh water and gentle soap (Dawn or Castile) or ½ strength peroxide and warm water. Gently pat area dry with a clean towel.

Then apply topical skin protecting crème such as over the counter anti-inflammatory/antibacterial crème. Gently apply thinly to affected area.

Keep grooming tools clean and disinfected. Proper stall hygiene is essential for horses suffering from rain rot. Rain rot is a contagious condition and will spread to other horses. Stalls must be mucked out daily.

Biting insects can spread rain rot so protecting from biting insects with fly blankets, leg wraps and fly masks should be considered. Maintaining proper manure management to reduce fly population is critical to decreasing the fly/insect population.

If you notice unusual discharge from the affected areas and/or your horse develops a fever, contact your veterinarian. Your horse will need an antibiotic to treat the bacterial infection.

Do not use ointments except on advice of veterinarian. Ointments tend to hold moisture and prevent skin from drying.

Thrush in Hooves

Thrush is a bacterial infection. It is also thought that yeast and fungal infections also contribute to a thrush infection. A thrush infection is fairly easy to identify by the black tar pus-like odoriferous discharge on the bottom of your horse's hoof. The presence of thrush is further confirmed when you experience a foul rank smell that would send a skunk running.

If the infection has penetrated sensitive tissues, the horse will react when the area is cleaned or pressed with a hoof pick. In severe cases, your horse can exhibit inflammation, tenderness, soreness and sometimes lameness.

Early detection usually makes it quite easy to treat and resolve thrush. If left untreated for a period of time, thrush can not only eat away the frog, but it can penetrate the sole and work its way into vital structures. Also, if left untreated for a period of time, the infection can be difficult to cure because most topical treatments can't reach all the deep nooks and crannies of the lower areas of the frog.

Thrush is often seen in horses that stand in muck and wet conditions. But, it is also found in horses with dry stabling. It can occur towards the end of a shoeing cycle when flaps of the frog grow over the sulci and trap dirt and moisture.

Again, the old adage of 'an ounce of prevention is worth a pound of cure' comes into play. This is so true when discussing hoof thrush infection. Daily hoof picking is a key to preventing thrush but be sure to really clean out the sulci rather than just picking out the sole. Regular exercise definitely contributes to overall hoof quality by increasing circulation. A clean dry environment helps prevent the organisms that cause thrush.

Have your farrier evaluate your horse's hooves if you suspect thrush. If the frog is overgrown your farrier will trim it. This will get rid of the infected part of the frog and allow air to circulate around the frog. If the frog isn't trimmed first, all the antibiotics in the world won't help.

After the frog is trimmed, clean the hoof by scrubbing the entire foot with a stiff brush and warm water. Wipe dry with clean dry towel. After allowing the foot to dry completely apply a topical thrush product. Any tack store, farm supply store or online horse supplier will offer a variety of thrush products. Consult with your veterinarian and/or farrier for advice on what works best for the particular conditions in your area.

Early detected thrush, after cleaning of the hoof and trimming of the frog, has been known to respond favourably to spraying infected area with apple cider vinegar or Listerine (original) mouthwash. Also soaking the affected foot daily in a bucket of warm water and Epson salts has garnered positive results. The use of Thrush Buster or Koppertox has also shown positive results.

Any treatment for mild thrush takes one or two weeks. Once improved, you will need to continue treatment for an additional two to three times a week until all signs of thrush are gone.

Some horse owners have used iodine for mild cases of thrush but even strong 7% iodine doesn't penetrate into the deep layers of the frog. Also it can dry out the hoof if used too often.

I was also advised by some that they used bleach as a good product for treating thrush. My own medical background made me question bleach as a treatment in this instance. I decided to research bleach so I could either confirm or rule it out as a viable treatment.

My concerns were validated. Bleach was ruled out as a good treatment option as it too can dry out the hoof and frog causing more damage than good. Bleach doesn't really kill the infection. Also bleach can cause significant damage to sensitive internal structures of the hoof if the thrush infection has created deep pockets of infection that lie next to the structures.

In conjunction with ongoing daily care, be sure to pick out the hooves every day. Keep your horse in a clean, dry environment until the problem clears up. Your horse doesn't have to be kept in a bedded stall, but be sure he has dry places to stand for most of the day.

Rubber mats can be a lifesaver for those who must contend with mud in winter and spring. Rubber mats not only offer a dry surface but a surface that is more pliable and forgiving for a tender foot. Once the thrush is cured, strive to maintain this dry, clean environment.

If your horse is troubled with frequent bouts of thrush consult your veterinarian and farrier.

Shedding

I'm sure there are those who will wonder why I would include this topic as an 'uncommon, common ailment' when shedding the 'winter coat' in the spring is such a natural event marking the end of winter and the coming of summer. It's common knowledge wearing a nylon jacket, shirt, etc over your clothes will keep you from presenting as a variation of Sassquash when you brush out that winter coat.

It's recommended that once or twice a week start with a shedding blade, then a rubber curry brush, then a hard bristle brush finishing with a soft brush. Using a grooming stone and proper grooming tools will stimulate shedding.

It can be a very major issue if your horse's coat does not shed. This is a very infrequent issue but, never-the-less worthy of discussion.

One method of determining if your horse's hair shedding is on track is to compare your horse to other horse's in the area. Some horses will delay hair loss when their bodies anticipate another cold snap. Then some horses are naturally behind with shedding and benefit from follicle stimulation through regular grooming and brushing.

If the majority of other horses around yours have naturally shed, then might need to consider what other reasons or issues might exist and influence the lack of shedding of your horse.

Horses with worms will often lack the ability to shed fully and on time. When this is the issue, horses that haven't shed on time will "blow" out their winter coat after deworming.

The temperature doesn't necessarily determine the coat shedding. Daylight and the length of days alert a horse's system when to shed hair as well.

If a horse is taken from a dark stall in the am and put back early evening in poorly/dim stalls, the horse's body will think it's still February. It's recommended to put your horse on a full turnout or adjust barn lighting to simulate midsummer by installing a timer to turn light on at 6 am and off at 10 pm.

Equine Cushing's disease can be detected from the condition of the horse's hair coat; anything from abnormal shedding to a wavy coat length. A common sign is a horse that fails to shed in the summer compiling a lengthy coat of hair. There are other symptoms that speak to Equine Cushing's disease.

I would highly recommend that you research Cushing Disease if you experience a shedding issue in your horse, especially if he/she is also experiencing increased urination and is an older horse.

Chapter XIII

"Nature does nothing uselessly."...Aristotle

Helpful Tips and Hints

Sprays for Flies, fleas, mosquitoes and ticks

I'm sure everyone has their own 'swear by' bug spray either store bought or homemade but I thought I would just share a few of my favourites with you. Have no real name for any of them so for reference purposes I'll just number them. I've identifed those that can be used on our dogs as well as 'all pets'.

Fly Spray #1   in a spray bottle mix

- 1 part white vinegar
- 1 part store-bought horse fly spray
  (use brand with permethrin .25% as active ingredient)

Shake well before each use and lasts just as long as normal.... about an hour or so.

Works just as well for house, stable and deer flies as when store-bought fly spray used alone. Since vinegar costs considerably less, this mixture saves money and gives equal or even better coverage.

Fly Spray #2   in a spray bottle mix

- 4 oz Skin-so-Soft
- 1 oz citronella oil
- 12 oz vinegar
- 12 oz water

Mix all together and spray on your horse. It remains effective as long as more expensive fly sprays and smells so much better. Bonus it's also very good for the coat.

SPECIAL NOTE: Recipe's call for citronella, use 100% pure citronella oil. It is a plant based product. Essential oils can be obtained in health foods stores, some drug stores or online suppliers.

Do Not Use citronella oil sold for use in outdoor torches. This oil is petroleum based with a citronella smell.

Fly spray #3   in a spray bottle mix

- 2 cups white vinegar
- 1 cup Avon Skin So Soft (Bath Oil)
- 1 cup water
- 1 tbsp eucalyptus oil

Mosquitoes Repellent #4 (also for ants and fleas)

Ingredients:
1/2 litre of alcohol
100 gram of whole cloves
100 ml of baby oil or similar oil (almond, sesame, chamomile, lavender, fennel etc)

Preparation:
Leave cloves to marinate in alcohol four days
Stir every morning and evening
After 4 days add the oil
It's now ready to use.

How to use:
Gently rub a few drops into the skin of the arms and legs.
Observe the mosquitoes fleeing the room.
Repels mosquito's and fleas on pets too including your horse.

Tick Spray #5   in a litre spray bottle mix

- 1 (one) part original Skin-so-Soft
- 1 (one) part Pine Sol
- 2 (two) parts water

Spray on your horse. Along with ticks, horse and deer flies are repelled as well.

Tick, Mosquitoes and Flea Spray #6 in a spray bottle mix

- 1 (one) part apple cider vinegar
- 1 (one) part water

Pour the solution in a spray bottle and spray directly onto your pets, but be careful not to get it in their eyes. If you have a horse, then the odds are in favour of you also having a dog. Works for your pets!

Tick, Mosquito, Fly spray #7 in a spray bottle mix

- 8 oz apple cider vinegar
- 4 oz warm water
- ½ tsp salt
- ½ tsp baking soda

Mix dry ingredients first then slowly add wet as the vinegar and baking soda will react slightly. Put into spray bottle and spray horses and pets down. Be careful not to get into eyes.

For dogs that live in the home, use Borax throughout the house by sprinkling it on the carpet; let sit for a few hours; then vacuum. This should kill fleas and ticks in your home and on your pets.

HOMEMADE MOSQUITO TRAP # 8 I use this system on my deck and at my stalls and it works just as well as those horrific mosquito coils.

Items needed:

- 1 cup of water
- 1/4 cup of brown sugar
- 1 gram of yeast
- 1 2-liter bottle

HOW:

1. Cut the plastic bottle in half.

2. Mix brown sugar with hot water. Let cool. When cold, pour in the bottom half of the bottle.

3. Add the yeast. No need to mix. It creates carbon dioxide, which attracts mosquitoes.

4. Place the funnel part, upside down, into the other half of the bottle, taping them together if desired.

Wrap the bottle with something black, leaving the top uncovered, and place it outside in an area away from your normal gathering area. (Mosquitoes are also drawn to the color black.) Change the solution every 2 weeks for continuous control. I call it my Hotel California. They can enter. They can just never leave.

Tick removal # 9

- Apply a small amount of Dawn original liquid soap on a cotton ball
- Cover the tick with the liquid soap cotton ball and gently rotate cotton ball counter clockwise for at least one minute.
- The tick will suffocate. The tick's grip is released into the soap soaked cotton ball or, by the misfortune of falling to the stall floor, dead or not receives a well deserved boot grinding.
- Can also use baby oil soaked cotton ball instead of Dawn soap

This truly does work. I've taken them off my horses and my dogs using this technique. Again it's a calm bonding moment of gentle rubbing and loving conversation. All is good.

Petroleum Jelly

Also known as vasoline is a stable in my stalls. I use it as a bug deterrent.

I use it to remove chestnuts off my appaloosa's legs. I smear the chestnuts daily for 5 – 7 days and then they peel off very easy. Everyone remains happy with easy.

During those winter months I use vasoline on the soles of my horses' hooves to prevent the packing of snow, ice or mud.

Pine tar can be removed by rubbing Vaseline into the mane and hair affected. In a few hours or the next day, it comes out easily with a clean dry cloth.

Mosquito/gnat control – my personal favourite. Mosquitoes and gnats enjoy the fine dining found under the tail, chin, throat, breast and genital area of your horse. I know they do with mine. It's a night out every night for these gluttonous critters.

I buy the dollar store petroleum jelly. I obtained a bottle of Diatomaceous Earth from my local Pet Value store. Diatomaceous Earth is an effective natural insecticide and dewormer for our pets that is sprinkled daily on their food. Diatomaceous Earth is the remains of microscopic one-celled plants that lived in the oceans and lakes that once covered parts of our earth and were left behind when the water receded. I don't give this to my horses in their feed. My dogs yes; my horses no.

For my horses I simply thoroughly mix one heaping tbsp of Diatomaceous Earth into an 8 oz jar of petroleum jelly. Before the first application I wash all the affected areas in order to eliminate the black sticky crusty deposits of gnats, flies, and little bumps from ticks. I then rub this on the cleansed surfaces. The unwanted critters have left. I find I have to repeat the process approximately every 4 – 5 days to discourage this dinner crowd from returning.

All though I have seen no adverse effects demonstrated by my babies, I urge everyone to do their own research and consulting before using any product, homeopathic or otherwise. I've seen no adverse effects demonstrated by my babies.

So far I'm winning this tug of war with no involvement of pesticides. I do have 3 horses that do not like the sound of the spray bottle nor do they appreciate the feel of the wet spray against their skin. But the no fuss no muss of having a rub down is always welcomed.

Apple Cider Vinegar (ACV) This is another staple at my stalls.

For those who prefer not to use insecticides for horse care, especially on foals less than 12 weeks old, make up your own vinegar based natural horse fly spray that you can rub or spray onto your horse's coat as needed.

Apple Cider Vinegar Fly Spray – in a spray bottle mix all ingredients well.

- 2 cups (500ml) apple cider vinegar (ACV)
- 1 cup (250 ml) water
- 1 cup (250 ml) Avon Skin so Soft (bath oil)
- 2 tsp (10 ml) Eucalyptus oil (or citronella oil)

While you're at it, you can make your own homemade vinegar fly trap for the barn, stalls or horse trailer.

Apple Cider Vinegar Fly Trap – punch holes in the lid of a large jar and the flies won't be able to fly out. Dissolve the sugar in the vinegar and water solution.

- 2 cups (500ml) water
- ¼ cup (60 ml) Apple Cider Vinegar
- ¼ cup (60 grams) sugar

Becomes yet another Hotel California for those uninvited quests!

Apple cider vinegar treatment for ringworm. Ringworm is an infection of the skin and hair by several types of fungi and <u>not</u> worms. Use full strength apple cider vinegar and rub it directly into the horse's skin around the ringworm infection. Rub in thoroughly two or three times a day for several consecutive days. Especially useful for ringworm infections that are too close to the eyes to use a copper wash.

Apple cider vinegar is an excellent treatment for thrush or other hoof fungal infections. Soak the affect hoof or hooves in a solution of ¼ cup (60 ml) of apple cider vinegar to one gallon (3.8 liters) of water for 10 – 15 minutes twice a day.

The vinegar application will, at the same time, speed up the healing of any other foot infections or bruises your horse might have.

Thrush and other foot fungus infections can be greatly reduced by a regular spray or soak application of apple cider vinegar to the sole and frog of your horse's feet. By making the hoof area more acidic, fungus is no longer able to grow well there.

Apple cider vinegar has been herald as a natural purifier for the drinking water of your horses as will destroy harmful microorganisms that can thrive in neutral or mildly basic water. Over two thousand years ago Roman soldiers would add vinegar to their drinking water for the same reasons.

It is considered horses will crib in search of the potassium in the wood. There has been success in decreasing this habit by adding to the drinking water apple cider vinegar for its potassium benefits.

Recommended dosage begins with from 1 cup (250ml) of apple cider vinegar (ACV) for every 50 gallons (190 liters) of drinking water all the way up to 1 cup (250 ml) for every 6 gallons (23 liters).

A trick commonly used for horses that will not drink the water in a new location is to add a little apple cider vinegar to unfamiliar water!

Because of its potassium and associated trace mineral content, this feed supplement is invaluable for mares coming up to foaling and it is also beneficial for older horses with digestive difficulties or arthritis.

For an otherwise healthy horse, use ¼ cup (60ml) of apple cider vinegar on his/her feed grain per day. Dilute the vinegar 50/50 with water before adding to the feed.

Chapter XIV

Some of my best leading men have been horses.....Elizabeth Taylor

Medical Records and Important Stuff

If you are boarding your horse or even if at your own property it is important to have your horse's normal vital signs readily available. In times of a stressful emergency this information will be of vital importance to your veterinarian when conducting an assessment of your horse's condition.

It is essential to know your horse's normal pulse, respiration rate and body temperature. Knowing what is normal for your horse is helpful if you need to determine if it is having respiratory problems or is developing a fever. You'll also be able to help the veterinarian, should your horse need treatment, by providing vital information accurately and quickly.

For quick access it would be prudent to write these values down together with a summary of your horses past and any present medical conditions. The name and telephone number of your veterinarian and farrier should also be with this information and everything kept at the stall for quick reference. A large zip lock bag holds this information quite nicely!

Normal Values: (these are general normal values)

- Pulse - 28 to 45 beats per minute (count the 'lub/dub' as one full beat)
- Respiration - 8 to 20 breaths per minute (regular rhythm)
- Temperature - 98.5F – 101F (36.9C – 38.3C)

Because these values are general normal ranges it would be advisable to check your horse over several days, at different times, to establish the normal ranges for your horse.

Air temperature can influence your horse's body temperature. Hot days can make the temperature increase slightly. Take the temp at cooler parts of the day and average the reading.

Exercise of any kind will increase the values. Even if your horse is anticipating a treat or suppertime, it may increase the pulse and respirations slightly. If your horse is very relaxed, you may get respirations as low as four breaths per minute.

Remember, when in doubt don't. If concerned at all call your veterinarian, and/or farrier for advice and guidance.

A very important thing to know is the weight of your horse. The only true accurate method is to use a proper weigh scale and for most of us that only happens if a trailer to the veterinarian is required.

The second best way is to use a 'heart girth weight' tape that can be purchased at most feed stores or tack shops and are relatively inexpensive. This tape will do the calculating for you based on the heart girth measurement. But it is not a precise measurement like a weigh scale.

The method most of will use will be with a regular cloth measuring tape using a formula that requires the measurement of the horse's heart girth and the horse's body length. That formula is 'heart girth X heart girth X length, divided by 330 + 75 = weight of your horse.

For example: if your horse's heart girth was 78" and his length was 65", the calculation would be: 78X78X65divided by 330 + 75 = 1,273 lbs approximate weight.

Measure heart girth: base of withers down to couple of inches behind the horse's front legs, under the belly and up the opposite side to where you started.

NOTE: tape measure will ran at an angle from front legs to withers.

Measuring body length: from the point of the shoulder to the point of the rump. The measurement you arrive at is your horse's length.

Or you can go on line where there are any number of horse sites that offer the use of their calculator based on your measurements of the heart girth and the body length of your horse.

You can then keep a weekly, monthly or yearly record of your horse's weight. The weight is so important when calculating feed rations, supplements and or medication. It's not 100% accurate but is much more accurate than just eye-balling and guesstimating.

Use this method when Blondie was having difficulty with the heaves. Worked sufficiently to give us the knowledge she was losing and then regaining her weight.

Conclusion

I thank you for reading my book. It is my most sincere hope that you found this book to be a source of valuable information, a refresher course of so much forgotten and a validation of all that you do know.

I want to thank all of my babies for all they have taught me. I have had most of them since they hit the ground. They know no life without me. It is a responsibility I gladly accept for the rewards I have received from knowing them all their life.

I started writing this book in the fall of 2012. It brought balance to my life when balance was hard to maintain. I got to immerse myself in the calming atmosphere of my horses' oneness with the universe and each other. They practiced order and have purpose to all they do. They offered an oasis of peace and harmony that presents unique ways of refusing entry to chaos.

During the writing of this book so much life has happened. Here at Cider River Ranch we lost two of our principle diva's. I am dedicating this book to them and my life long friend Jane.

On December 1, 2014 we lost our Blondie. She had been having difficulty with her spine and hip for almost a year. With equine chiropractor visits, physiotherapy and medications things were starting to get better. On December 1, 2014 the barn yard was very muddy. Blondie slipped and fell hard onto the bad hip. We all miss her so much. She is forever owed a debt of gratitude for her kind, patient, tolerant forgiving nature. One of a kind and we are so grateful she was ours.

March 2015 my life long friend Jane passed away. I miss her. I am forever grateful for her supportive friendship through all life's changes. She too was one of a kind and I am so grateful she was my friend.

October 2015 we lost our Miss Missy. It still remains too painful. She was my farm buddy and my stall buddy. Words can't begin to express the loss we all feel. Missy was the family dog. She represented different things to different people in different ways but to each of us she was always just Missy. One of a kind and we are so grateful she was ours.

I initially wanted to create treat recipes to accommodate my fatty patties and hunkie chunkies only to realize treats were not the culprit. They didn't get enough, frequently enough for that to have an impact. That is when this incredible journey born of the need to know morphed into Creature Comforts for Horses.

Again it is my most sincere hope you found this book to be a source of valuable information, a refresher course of so much forgotten and a validation of all that you do know. I know it was for me.

Callie Palomino and Apache Appoloosa

the end

"Horses change lives. They give our young people confidence and self-esteem. They provide peace and tranquility to troubled souls, they give us hope." ....Toni Robinson

Acknowledgement

My first words of appreciation and gratitude belong to a loving God that showed me he does not closed one door but that He opens another.

I thank God for ensuring my path was endowed with the most amazing people he could find to assist me while writing my book. I thank God for the ability to put into words the creature comfort needs of my horses so that I could pay it forward to others who share the same devoted love affair with their horses.

I am grateful for the support and encouragement of my adult children, Samuel, Stephan & Sheighlyn. To Tyler, my chosen son, words can't begin to express how grateful I am for your unquestionable encouragement, support and, from to time, bridge financing of my creature comfort needs during the four years of writing this book.

To my circle of friends who gave generously & willingly of their time, support, encouragement and wise council my most heartfelt thank you and overwhelming appreciation.

I know I have been blessed when God aligned my star with yours.

In particular my profound thank you to my sister Alberta Mae Ayers, Jane Sloan, Brian Spenser, Elise Van Schaik, Betty Barker, Christine Cousins, Janet Kirvan, Louise & Fred Kowal (my Saskatchewan friends who introduced me to my horse addiction), David & Gail Rockford (my call a friend when horse sense required), Jennifer Ryan (my RBC financial advisor extraordinaire), Allison Davis (who planted the seed to write the book), Michelle Ryder, Grant Stoval for the beautiful pictures, Geoff Gardiner for the dynamic logo and Andrew Yongenotter (the man with the hay) and most favoured by my horses.

From the bottom of my heart and those of Blondie, Foxy, Apache, PJ, Roxy, Callie, Catman & Chance, our most sincere thank you.....couldn't have done this without you. God bless you all.